T0337621

Vom Nutzen der Architekturfotografie
Positionen zur Beziehung von Bild und Architektur

Architectural Photography and Its Uses
Positions on the Relationship between Image and Architecture

Angelika Fitz, Gabriele Lenz
mit with ig-architekturfotografie (Hg. / Ed.)

Birkhäuser
Basel

Einleitung
Introduction

Eine Publikation mit dem Titel *Vom Nutzen der Architekturfotografie* tritt in große Fußstapfen. Die Anspielung auf eine bedeutende philosophische Abhandlung[1] ist ernst gemeint und zugleich mit einem Zwinkern versehen. Ernst ist es den Herausgeberinnen mit ihrem Anliegen, das Verhältnis von Fotografie und Architektur ganz grundsätzlich zu untersuchen. Die Art und Weise, wie die Architekturfotografie unsere Beziehung zur gebauten Umwelt prägt, ist noch wenig erforscht. Wenn es darum geht, „ein Verständnis für die jeweils vorherrschenden historischen Verhältnisse zwischen Architektur, Nutzung, Ökonomie, Politik, Raum, Ort und Handlung zu erlangen", so Elke Krasny in ihrem Buchbeitrag, „enthalten Architekturfotografien die entscheidenden Hinweise".[2] Es gilt also, genau hinzusehen, und dafür bietet die vorliegende Publikation in zehn Kapiteln reichlich Gelegenheit. Was auf den ersten Blick wie ein kurzweiliger Bilderreigen anmutet, ist gleichzeitig eine Analyse mit visuellen Mitteln. In zehn Episoden berichten die Fotografien von ihrem Verhältnis zur Architektur und von den gesellschaftlichen Verhältnissen, in denen Architektur produziert, genutzt und vermittelt wird. Die Fotografien kommentieren sich in der Hauptsache gegenseitig, auch wenn sie hier und da von Textkommentaren begleitet werden. Sie erlauben Sichtwechsel. Sie zeigen, welchen Unterschied der Kontext macht, sei es der landschaftliche oder der gebaute, die beide immer auch ökonomische und politische Kontexte sind. Sie führen vor, wie Fotografinnen und Fotografen die Architektur für ihre eigenen Geschichten nutzen und wie die Fotografien in den Architekturmedien genutzt werden.

Die zehn Episoden decken ein breites Themenspektrum ab, von Fragen der medialen Erfolgskriterien über Formen der Künstlichkeit und Alltäglichkeit bis zum Verhältnis von Menschen und Räumen. Zusammengehalten werden sie durch das Motiv des Nutzens: „Nutzungsspuren", „Nutzungsbeziehungen", „Vom Nutzen des Standpunkts", „Vom Nutzen der Wiedererkennbarkeit", „Vom Nutzen der Mittel" oder „Nach der Nutzung" – so lauten die Untertitel der Episoden. Und damit sind wir bei der spielerischen Aneignung des mächtigen Titels: Die Figur des Nutzers oder der Nutzerin ist ein genuin architektonisches Motiv.[3] Lange bevor das digitale Zeitalter seinen „User" hervorbrachte, produzierte die Architektur den Nutzer. Mit dem Konzept des Nutzers wird das Verhalten der Menschen als vorhersehbar konstruiert. Die Komplexität des

A publication that bears the title *Architectural Photography and Its Uses* is following in some rather substantial footsteps. The allusion to an important philosophical treatise[1] is meant to be a serious one, albeit accompanied by a wink. But the editors are serious, too, about their aim, which is to submit the relationship between photography and architecture to a fundamental investigation. To date, the ways in which architectural photography conditions our relationship to the built environment have only been researched to a minimal degree. When it comes to arriving at "an understanding of the historical relations that prevailed respectively between architecture, use, economics, politics, space, place, and action," writes Elke Krasny in her contribution to this collection, "it is architectural photography that provides us with the decisive references…"[2] It is a question, then, of looking with precision, and the present publication in ten chapters offers a wealth of opportunities for doing so. That which at first glance resembles a diverting series of images is also an analysis that deploys visual resources. In ten episodes, the photographs reveal their relationship to architecture and to the social relations through which architecture is produced, used, and mediated. For the most part, the photographs comment on one another reciprocally even when they are occasionally provided with textual annotations. They make shifts of perspective possible. They demonstrate the importance of context; whether a landscape or a built environment, both consistently constitute an economic and a political framework. They demonstrate the ways in which photographers use architecture to tell their own stories and how photographs are deployed by the architectural media.

The ten episodes cover a broad thematic spectrum, from criteria of media success, to forms of artificiality and the everyday, to the relationship between human beings and spaces. Unity is generated by the motif of use. "Traces of Use," "Relations of Use," "On the Uses of Viewpoint," "On the Uses of Recognizability," "On the Use of Resources," "After Use," so read the subtitles of the various episodes. And at this point we have come to the playful appropriation of the formidable title, i.e., the figure of the user is a genuinely architectural motif.[3] Long before the digital age had generated its "user," architecture had already produced the user. With the

Angelika Fitz

menschlichen Lebens wird auf einen planbaren Bezug zum Raum reduziert. Viele Architekturfotografien in diesem Buch zeigen Situationen außerhalb dieser Vorgabe. Die Menschen auf den Fotografien brechen aus der für sie vorgesehene Rolle aus. Nutzungsspuren verraten, dass die Architektur unsachgemäß verwendet wurde. Nutzerinnen und Nutzer erobern Räume und verlassen sie – nicht immer nach Plan.

Die Frage des Nutzens regelt aber nicht nur die Beziehung zwischen Mensch, Plan und Raum, sondern auch die Beziehung zwischen Investor und Architekturbüro, und nicht zuletzt jene zwischen Architektur und Fotografie. Ähnlich wie die Architektur wird auch die Architekturfotografie von Diskussionen über ihren Nutzen zwischen Dienstleistung und Kunst begleitet. Sie dient einerseits der medialen Vervielfältigung, Vermittlung und Archivierung von Bauwerken und prägt andererseits durch ihren ästhetischen Eigensinn ein spezifisches Bild der gebauten Wirklichkeit. Die vorliegende Publikation beleuchtet beide Ebenen. Einerseits widmen sich die Bildstrecken dem Thema „Nutzung als Inhalt der Architekturfotografie". Welche Beiträge leistet die Architekturfotografie zu Fragen des Gebrauchs von Architektur? Wann werden Bauwerke im Ursprungszustand dokumentiert; wann und wie werden sie in der Nutzung gezeigt? Andererseits untersucht *Vom Nutzen der Architekturfotografie*, wie die Fotografien selbst genutzt werden. Nach welchen Kriterien suchen Architekturmagazine Bilder aus? Welche Fotografien bringen Quote, welche bringen neue Blickwinkel? Daran anschließend wird die Frage gestellt, wie Architektinnen und Architekten die Fotografie für ihre Zwecke einsetzen. In der Architekturgeschichte kennt man Werkserien, die eng mit der Handschrift einzelner Fotografinnen und Fotografen verbunden sind. Die Fotografie ist nicht nur Vermittlerin der Architekturgeschichte, sondern trägt aktiv dazu dabei, einen Stil oder eine ganze Epoche zu prägen.

Gerade in Zeiten der Bilderflut, in der sich Renderings – computergenerierte Visualisierungen, die in den letzten Jahren immer detailgetreuer geworden sind – kaum mehr von Fotografien unterscheiden lassen, will das Projekt *Vom Nutzen der Architekturfotografie* den kulturellen Wert der Architekturfotografie umfassend untersuchen. Initiiert wurde diese Recherche von der ig-architekturfotografie, einer Interessensgemeinschaft von Fotografinnen und Fotografen, die 2003 in Österreich gegründet wurde. In Österreich ist in den letzten Jahrzehnten eine facettenreiche

concept of the user, human behavior is defined as predictable. The complexity of human life is reduced to relationships to space that can be planned out. Many architectural photographs found in this book show situations that reside outside of such parameters. The people in the photographs break with the roles that have been envisioned for them. Traces of use betray the ways in which architecture is "improperly" used. Users appropriate spaces and then abandon them – and not always according to plan.

But the question of use not only regulates the relationship between the human individual, the plan, and space but also that between the investor and the architectural practice and, not least of all, between architecture and photography. Not unlike architecture, architectural photography is accompanied by discussions touching on its uses, which lie somewhere between providing a service and art. On the one hand, it serves media reproduction, dissemination, and archiving of buildings, while on the other, its esthetic intransigence leaves its mark on a specific image of built reality. The present publication illuminates both levels. First, the image sequence is devoted to the theme of "Use as the Content of Architectural Photography". What contributions does architectural photography make to the questions surrounding the use of architecture? When are buildings documented in their original conditions? When and how are they depicted in use? On the other hand, *Architectural Photography and Its Uses* investigates the ways in which photography itself is used. According to which criteria do architectural magazines select images? Which photographs generate greater readership, and which bring new perspectives? This leads to the question of how architects deploy photography for their own purposes. Recognizable in architectural history are series of works that are closely bound up with the trademark approach of a certain photographer. The photographer is not only a mediator of architectural history but contributes to it actively by defining a style or even an entire epoch.

Precisely in a time characterized by a perpetual flood of images, when renderings – computer-generated visualizations that have become increasingly detailed in recent years – are barely distinguishable from photographs, the project *Architectural Photography and Its*

architekturfotografische Szene entstanden, die nicht nur mit der vielfälti-
gen heimischen Architekturlandschaft zusammenarbeitet, sondern
international tätig ist. Im Entstehungsprozess der Publikation bildeten die
Mitglieder der ig-architekturfotografie eine temporäre Arbeitsgemein-
schaft mit der Gestalterin Gabriele Lenz sowie mit mir selbst als Kuratorin
und Kulturtheoretikerin. Erste, kuratorisch gesetzte Themen forderten
die Fotografinnen und Fotografen dazu auf, ihre Archive zu durchforsten
und die eigenen Interessen, Herangehensweisen, Arbeitsbedingungen
und Ansprüche zu reflektieren. Das ausgehobene Material umfasst
sowohl Auftragsarbeiten als auch freie künstlerische Arbeiten aus den
letzten Jahrzehnten, wobei der Schwerpunkt in der jüngeren Vergangenheit und der Gegenwart liegt. Die Sichtung der vorgeschlagenen
Arbeiten erweiterte und präzisierte die Episodenstruktur und führte teilweise in Rückkoppelungsschleifen zu weiteren Bildvorschlägen, die
wiederum kuratorisch verarbeitet wurden. In diesem Sinne ist *Vom Nutzen
der Architekturfotografie* ein „arbeitendes Buch", das als kollektives
„work-in-progress" viele Autorinnen und Autoren hat. Auswahl der Fotografien, Zusammenstellung der Bildserien und visuelle Gestaltung
greifen dabei eng ineinander: Erst auf der Analysefläche der Buchseiten
lassen sich die Argumente, die in der Hauptsache visuell vorgetragen
werden, überprüfen.

Eingebunden in das Verfahren des arbeitenden Buches waren auch
Architektinnen und Architekten sowie Architekturvermittlerinnen und
-vermittler. Mit ihren Kommentaren, die sich direkt auf einzelne Fotografien und deren Entstehungsgeschichte beziehen, machen sie deutlich,
dass Architekturfotografie weit über das Dokumentarische hinausgeht.
Architektinnen und Architekten erklären, weshalb sie mit bestimmten
Fotografinnen und Fotografen zusammenarbeiten. Journalistinnen und
Journalisten geben Einblicke in ihre Auswahlkriterien. Kuratorinnen und
Kuratoren reflektieren die kulturelle Einengung der Sehgewohnheiten
und protestieren gleichzeitig dagegen. Theoretikerinnen und Theoretiker
erklären, dass es weniger um die Beherrschung der technischen Appa-
ratur geht als um die spezifische Sichtweise. Und ein Schriftsteller sucht
Parallelen zwischen Fotografie und literarischer Arbeit.

Eingeleitet wird die visuelle Analyse von zwei Essays, die, obwohl
von zwei verschiedenen Richtungen beginnend, beide zu einem ähnlichen

Uses strives to explore the cultural value of architectural
photography in a comprehensive way. Our research
was initiated by ig-architekturfotografie, an association
of photographers founded in Austria in 2003. In recent
decades, a multifaceted scene for architectural
photography has emerged in Austria, one that not only
collaborates with the highly diverse domestic architectural landscape but is also active internationally. In the
process that eventually yielded this publication, the
members of ig-architekturfotografie formed a temporary
working group with the designer Gabriele Lenz, along
with the present author as curator and cultural theoretician. Initial, curatorially defined themes invited the
photographers to go through their archives and reflect
upon their own interests, approaches, working conditions, and standards. The material they dug out encom-
passes both commissioned works and autonomous
images from the last few decades with an emphasis on
the recent past and the present. A selection from among
the proposed works expanded and refined the structure
of the episodes and to some extent led to a feedback
loop that generated proposals for additional images,
which were in turn processed in curatorial terms. In this
sense, *Architectural Photography and Its Uses* is a
"working book" that has, as a collective work in progress,
multiple authors. The choice of photographs, the configuration of the series of images, and the visual design
are closely intertwined. Only the analytical space of the
book's pages examines the arguments, which are for
the most part presented visually.

Architects were integrated into the processes of
this working book along with architectural intermediaries.
The commentaries, which refer directly to the individual photographs and their origins, clearly show that
architectural photography transcends the documentary.
The architects explain why they chose to collaborate
with specific photographers. Journalists offer insights
into their criteria of selection. Curators reflect upon
cultural limitations and visual habits while protesting
against them. Theoreticians explain that it is less a
question of mastering the technical apparatus than of
a particular mode of seeing. And a writer searches for
parallels between photography and literary work.

The visual analysis is introduced by two essays
which – despite differing points of departure – arrived

Schluss kommen: Architekturfotografie bildet die kulturellen, ökonomischen und politischen Kontexte nicht nur ab, sondern formt sie aktiv mit. Wie Philip Ursprung beschreibt, wird die Architekturfotografie dabei nicht nur zur Komplizin der Architekturgeschichte, sondern hält ihr auch einen kritischen Spiegel vor. So sei es seit den Anfängen der Architekturfotografie ein wiederkehrendes Motiv, die Transformation der Städte zu dokumentieren, von den Haussmann'schen Eingriffen in Paris bis zu den Megalopolen im heutigen China; quasi ein kollektives Langzeitprojekt, das die Wirkungskräfte des Kapitalismus vom 19. bis zum 21. Jahrhundert veranschaulicht. Elke Krasny widmet sich in ihrem Text der Schlüsselrolle, die die Fotografie bei der Konstruktion des Diskurses über die Moderne gespielt hat. Der strahlende Bilderkanon beruhe auf dem Ausschluss der Rückseite der Moderne. Abgebildet würde die Vorderseite des fordistischen Kapitalismus, während informelle Nutzungen und Reproduktionsarbeit ausgeblendet blieben. Dem stellt sie zwei Beispiele ephemerer Architektur gegenüber, räumliche Situationen abseits eines wirtschaftlichen Verwertungszusammenhanges, und zeigt, wie hier in der Fotografie die Gebäude zugunsten der Nutzungen in den Hintergrund treten.

Damit sollte deutlich geworden sein, dass die Frage nach dem Nutzen der Architekturfotografie grundlegende Fragen zur Beziehung zwischen Architektur und Fotografie umfasst, ebenso wie jene nach dem Verhältnis zwischen Ökonomie und Architektur oder zwischen Medien und Fotografie. Das Resultat ist eine Publikation, die das Zusammenwirken von Fotografie und Architektur sichtbar macht, Einblicke hinter die Kulissen der Architekturfotografie gibt und nicht zuletzt exzellente Beispiele österreichischer Architekturfotografie versammelt. Erkenntnisgewinn und Schauvergnügen gehen dabei, so hoffe ich, Hand in Hand.

at similar conclusions: Architectural photography not only depicts cultural, economic, and political contexts, it actively shapes them at the same time. As Philip Ursprung demonstrates, architectural photography, while it becomes an accessory to architectural history, also holds up a critical mirror to it. Since its inception, one recurring motif of architectural photography has been the need to document the transformation of cities, from Haussmann's interventions in Paris all the way to the megalopolises of contemporary China, a collective long-term project of sorts, one that visualizes the consequences of capitalism all the way from the 19th to the 21st centuries. Elke Krasny's essay is devoted to the key role photography has played in constructing the discourses of modernity. The resplendent canon of images, she argues, rests on the exclusion of the reverse of modernity, its rear side. Represented instead is the front side of Fordist capitalism, while informal uses and reproductive work remain shielded from view. In opposition to this, she presents two examples of ephemeral architecture, spatial situations that are located beyond contexts of economic valorization, and shows how in these instances, photography allows the building to retreat into the background in favor of its utilization.

All of this should demonstrate that a discussion of the uses of architectural photography must encompass the fundamental questions concerning the relationship between architecture and photography, economics and architecture, and the media and photography. The result is a publication that sheds light on forms of cooperation between photography and architecture, offers a glimpse behind the scenes at photographic practices vis-à-vis architecture, and, last but not least, brings together superb examples of Austrian architectural photography. It is my hope that here the insights to be had and visual pleasure go hand-in-hand.

1 Gemeint ist Friedrich Nietzsches Abhandlung „Vom Nutzen und Nachteil der Historie für das Leben" (1874); siehe dazu auch den Text von Philip Ursprung in dieser Publikation, S. 13.
2 Elke Krasny, „Von der Nutzung der Architektur in der Fotografie" in dieser Publikation, S. 31.
3 Darauf hat zuletzt Elke Krasny bei der BINA-Konferenz *Citizens and City Making* im Mai 2015 in Belgrad hingewiesen.

1 The German-language title of this volume, *Vom Nutzen der Architekturfotografie*, plays on the title of Friedrich Nietzsche's essay "Vom Nutzen und Nachteil der Historie für das Leben" (1874), which is familiar to English readers as "On the Use and Abuse of History for Life." Cf. also Philip Ursprung's text in the present publication, pp. 13.
2 Elke Krasny, "On the Use of Architecture in Photography," pp. 31 in the present publication.
3 Elke Krasny recently called attention to this motif at the BINA conference *Citizens and City Making* held in Belgrade in May of 2015.

Tragbare Räume
Portable Spaces

Der Himmel über dem Gebauten spielt in der Architekturfotografie eine wichtige Rolle. Dabei geht es nicht nur um ästhetische Entscheidungen, sondern auch um ganz pragmatische Begleiterscheinungen wie Sonne, Wolken und Niederschläge – das Cover-Sujet dieses Buches bezieht sich darauf. Es ist mehr grau als blau, und trotz der Wolken bildet der Himmel über dem Theseustempel im Wiener Volksgarten einen annähernd monochromen Hintergrund für den Buchtitel. Material und Farbe des Covers beziehen sich auch auf den Leineneinband des Buches *Form* von Max Bill aus dem Jahr 1952. Das wichtige Standardwerk zur Designgeschichte erschien als Leinenband in meliertem Hellblau.

Der gestalterische Anspruch an heutige Fotobücher ist nicht ohne den Rückblick auf die Entwicklung der modernen Buchgestaltung zu sehen. Die Verwendung von Fotografien in Büchern und eine erneuerte Gestaltung des Mediums gingen Hand in Hand. 1923 ans Bauhaus in Weimar berufen, prägte László Moholy-Nagy das Erscheinen der Hauspublikationen und setzte sich in Theorie und Praxis dafür ein, Fotos als vollwertige Komponenten bildhafter typografischer Kompositionen zu betrachten.[1] Die Gestaltungsanforderungen des Bauhauses wurden zugleich inhaltlich vermittelt und in der Gestaltung der Bücher umgesetzt. Bei der traditionsverhafteten Zunft der Buchkünstler und Typografen stand man Fotos in Büchern sehr reserviert gegenüber und verwies das Foto in den Bereich des Journalismus.[2] Der junge Typograph Jan Tschichold, beeinflusst durch den Aufsatz „Neue Typografie" von László Moholy-Nagy, sah das anders. Er gab 1929 mit Franz Roh das Buch *Foto-Auge. 76 Fotos der Zeit* mit Fotografien von Andreas Feiningner, John Heartfield, Florence Henri, Moholy-Nagy, Man Ray und anderen heraus.[3] Für die Gestaltung konnte Tschichold seine neuen Ideen für Text-Bild-Kompositionen umsetzen. Er beschreibt den sich verändernden Stellenwert der Fotografie so: „das foto ist zu einem so bezeichnenden merkmal unserer zeit geworden, daß man es sich nicht mehr hinwegdenken könnte." Außerdem thematisiert er den „bildhunger des modernen menschen".[4]

Einen wichtigen Beitrag zur Entwicklung des modernen Architekturbuchs realisierten 1927 der Architekt Bruno Taut, der Typograf Johannes Molzahn und der Fotograf Arthur Köster.[5] Molzahn gestaltete nicht nur nach den Prinzipien der „Neuen Typografie"; entscheidend war, dass er hier erstmals mit dem „Buchkinema" einen völlig neuen Umgang mit den

In architectural photography, the skies above the buildings play an important role. It is a question not simply of esthetic decisions, but also of entirely pragmatic ancillary visual phenomena such as sunlight, clouds, and precipitation – to which the cover motif of this publication alludes. More gray than blue, and despite the clouds, the sky above the Theseus Temple in Vienna's Volksgarten provides an almost monochrome background for the book's title. The materiality and color of the cover allude to the cloth binding of Max Bill's book *Form*, published in 1952. This important standard work on design history appeared as a hardcover volume in mottled pale blue.

The design aspirations of contemporary photobooks cannot be considered without a retrospective glance at the development of modern book design. The use of photographs in books and the renewal of the medium went hand in hand. Appointed to the Bauhaus in Weimar in 1923, László Moholy-Nagy shaped the appearance of the school's house publications and committed himself in theory and in practice to treating photographs as fully fledged components of pictorially conceived typographic compositions.[1] The design demands of the Bauhaus were conveyed through content as well as the book's design. The guild of book artists and typographers, with its strong attachment to tradition, regarded the use of photographs in books with reservations, consigning the medium to the realm of journalism.[2] The young typographer Jan Tschichold, influenced by Moholy-Nagy's essay "The New Typography," saw things differently. In 1929, he and Franz Roh edited the book *Foto-Auge. 76 Fotos der Zeit (Photo Eye: 76 Photos of the Time)*, with photographs by Andreas Feininger, John Heartfield, Florence Henri, Moholy-Nagy, Man Ray, and others.[3] For the design, Tschichold implemented his new ideas for text-image composition. He characterized the altered status of photography as follows, "The photograph has become such a characteristic sign of the times that our lives would be unthinkable without it." He also thematized the "modern man's hunger for images".[4]

An important contribution to the development of the modern architectural book was made in 1927 by the architect Bruno Taut, the typographer Johannes Molzahn, and the photographer Arthur Köster.[5] Molzahn executed his design according to the principles of the "New Typography"; his way was decisive, cultivating

Gabriele Lenz

Abbildungen pflegte.[6] Er verfolgte die Idee einer filmartigen Anordnung von Fotografien, „die einen sich bewegenden Betrachter simulieren sollte und damit Raum, Architektur und Betrachter über das Medium des Buchs vereinen sollte".[7] Die Verbindung von Architektur, Fotografie und Buch hat besonders der Architekt Le Corbusier in seiner umfangreichen Publikationstätigkeit gestärkt.[8] In ihm sah der Fotograf Lucien Hervé ab dem Ende der 1940er-Jahre ein Gegenüber, das wie er selbst an der Entwicklung einer modernen Ästhetik arbeitete. Hervés Bilder von Le Corbusiers Bauten sind Dokumentation und eigenständiges Werk zugleich.[9]

Unverändert seit seinem Bestehen ist das Buch als physisches Objekt, ein in Format und Umfang abgegrenzter, endlicher Raum in einer Abfolge von Doppelseiten. Der Vergleich mit einer Ausstellung und der kuratorischen Arbeit bei der Auswahl der Bilder und deren Anordnung liegt nahe; auch im Unterschied zur Prozesshaftigkeit der Bildfolgen im Internet, die ein indifferentes Bilderrauschen erzeugen. Das Buch erfordert eine konzentrierte Reduktion, eine räumliche Gegenüberstellung des Bildmaterials und, vor dem Hintergrund der Unveränderbarkeit, eine dauerhafte inhaltliche und gestalterische Struktur. Fotografien auf Buchseiten materialisieren sich mehrheitlich im Offsetdruck auf Papier, einem dreidimensionalen Trägermedium. Dieses beeinflusst die Wirkung der Fotos und transferiert sie ins Buch. Durch das Umblättern entsteht eine Bewegung im Raum und lässt die Seiten und das darauf Gedruckte beim Blättern perspektivisch erscheinen. Die Buchseiten mögen zweidimensional wirken – durch das Umblättern der Seiten entsteht ein Bilderraum. Gleichzeitig ist das Buch als Objekt in diesem Fall ein beweglicher Raum für Architekturfotografie.

an entirely new treatment of the illustrations with the so-called "book cinema."[6] He pursued the idea of a filmic arrangement of photographs that would "simulate the moving observer, thereby unifying space, the architecture, and the viewer via the medium of the book".[7] It was the architect Le Corbusier in particular who was invigorated in his wide-ranging publishing activities by the conjunction of architecture, photography, and the book.[8] As of the late 1940s, the photographer Lucien Hervé regarded Le Corbusier as a confrère committed to the development of a modernist esthetic. Hervé's images of Le Corbusier's buildings are simultaneously forms of documentation and autonomous works.[9]

As a physical object, the book has remained unaltered since its genesis, delimited in form and extent, a finite space within a sequence of facing pages. With regard to the selection of images and their configuration, the design of books lends itself to comparisons with exhibitions and curatorial work. Both contrast with the process-oriented character of image sequences found on the Internet, which produce an indifferent flood of images. A book per se calls for a concentrated reduction, a spatially defined juxtaposition of pictorial material, and, in light of its immutability, an enduring design in terms of content and structure. For the most part, photographs on the pages of books are materialized as offset printing on paper, a three-dimensional supporting medium. This influences the impact of the photographs and transfers them into the book. Turning a book's page produces a movement in space that makes those very pages and the images printed on them appear perspectival. The pages of the book may seem two-dimensional, but as we turn them over, a kind of image space emerges. And at the same time, the book – as object – is a space for architectural photography that can be set in motion.

1, 2 Claudia Müller, *Typofoto: Wege der Typographie zur Foto-Text-Montage bei László Moholy-Nagy*, Gebrüder Mann, 1994.
3 Franz Roh und Jan Tschichold, *foto-auge/œil et photo/photo-eye*, Akademischer Verlag, Stuttgart, 1929.
4 Jan Tschichold, „Fotografie und Typografie" in: *Die Form, Zeitschrift für gestaltende Arbeit*, Verlag Hermann Reckendorf, Berlin, 1928, Heft 5, S. 140.
5 Es handelt sich um das eigene Haus des Architekten: *Bruno Taut, Ein Wohnhaus. Mit 104 Fotos und 72 Zeichnungen, einer Farbaufnahme und einer Farbzusammenstellung*, Stuttgart, 1927.
6 Matthias Noell, *Das Haus und sein Buch*, Basel, 2009, S. 32.
7 Johannes Molzahn, „Nicht mehr Lesen! Sehen!", in: *Das Kunstblatt*, Jg. 12, 1928, S. 78–82.
8 Catherine de Smet, *Le Corbusier, Architekt der Bücher*, Lars Müller Publishers, Baden, 2007.
9 Le Corbusier, Lucien Hervé, *Kontakte*, Schirmer/Mosel, München, 2011.

1, 2 Claudia Müller, *Typofoto: Wege der Typographie zur Foto-Text-Montage bei László Moholy-Nagy*, Gebrüder Mann, 1994.
3 Franz Roh and Jan Tschichold, *foto-auge/œil et photo/photo-eye*, Akademischer Verlag, Stuttgart, 1929.
4 Jan Tschichold, "Photography and Typography," in: *Photography in the Modern Era: European Documents and Critical Writings, 1913–1940*, Christopher Phillips (ed.), Aperture Books, New York, 1989, p. 122. (Originally published as "Fotografie und Typografie," *Die Form, Zeitschrift für gestaltende Arbeit*, 5 Berlin, 1928, p. 140.)
5 It was the architect's own home that was depicted: *Bruno Taut, Ein Wohnhaus. Mit 104 Fotos und 72 Zeichnungen, einer Farbaufnahme und einer Farbzusammenstellung*, Stuttgart, 1927.
6 Matthias Noell, *Das Haus und sein Buch*, Basel, 2009, p. 32.
7 Johannes Molzahn, *"Nicht mehr Lesen! Sehen!"* in: *Das Kunstblatt* 12, 1928, pp. 78–82.
8 Catherine de Smet, *Le Corbusier, Architect of Books*, Lars Müller Publishers, Baden, 2007.
9 Le Corbusier, Lucien Hervé, *Kontakte*, Schirmer/Mosel, Munich, 2011.

Vom Nutzen und Nachteil der
Fotografie für die Architektur
On the Use and Abuse of
Photography for Architecture

Philip Ursprung

Als Friedrich Nietzsche 1874 seine berühmte Abhandlung "Vom Nutzen und Nachteil der Historie für das Leben" als Teil der *Unzeitgemäßen Betrachtungen* veröffentlichte, war die Frage nach der Rolle der Geschichte eine der zentralen Fragen seiner Zeit. Es ging um die Spannung zwischen der Historie, also dem Bewusstsein der Zeitlichkeit, und dem Leben im Hier und Jetzt. Nietzsche legte die Vorteile und vor allem auch die Gefahren dar, die die Konzentration auf die Geschichtlichkeit für seine Zeitgenossen in den Bereichen der Politik, der Moral und der Wissenschaft darstellte. Wenn heute die Frage nach dem Nutzen der Architekturfotografie aufgeworfen wird, kann diese natürlich nicht dieselbe Tragweite für sich beanspruchen wie Nietzsches damalige Frage zum Verhältnis von Vergangenheit und Gegenwart. Aber sie richtet das Augenmerk auf die Definition von Architektur und ist daher für alle, die sich mit dieser Thematik auseinandersetzen, relevant.

Bereits das in der Frage implizite Abwägen, ob die Architekturfotografie der Architektur nutze oder schade, legt nahe, dass das Verhältnis zwischen Architektur und Fotografie nicht statisch, sondern dynamisch ist. Meine These ist, dass das Verhältnis zwischen Architektur und Fotografie immer dann ins Zentrum des Interesses rückt, wenn sich eine oder beide Gattungen verändern. Generell ist die Beobachtung des Bereichs zwischen verschiedenen Gattungen – zum Beispiel zwischen Kunst und Architektur, Skulptur und Malerei, Skulptur und Performance – fruchtbar, weil dieser ein Indikator für eine Transformation ist. So drängt sich die Untersuchung der Beziehung zwischen Fotografie und Architektur auf, weil dabei Abläufe ins Licht rückten, die verborgen bleiben, wenn man die Geschichte von Architektur und Fotografie getrennt betrachtet.

Die Beziehung zwischen Fotografie und Architektur reicht bis in die 1830er-Jahre zurück, in denen die Fotografie erfunden wurde. Es ist ein Klischee, dass die Architektur sich als Motiv der Fotografie gerade deshalb besonders gut eigne, weil Gebäude sich nicht bewegen. Diese Vorstellung greift meiner Meinung nach jedoch zu kurz, denn für die Fotografie sind ja gerade diejenigen Gegenstände attraktiv, die sich verändern und vergänglich sind. Ich behaupte, dass die Beziehung zwischen der noch jungen Fotografie und der Architektur nicht deshalb so eng war, weil die Architektur sich für lange Belichtungszeiten eignet – in dem Fall müsste auch eine besonders nahe Beziehung zwischen Fotografie und

In 1874, when Friedrich Nietzsche published his celebrated essay "Vom Nutzen und Nachteil der Historie für das Leben" (originally translated as "On the Use and Abuse of History for Life") as part of his *Unzeitgemäße Betrachtungen (Untimely Meditations)*, the role of history represented an essential question for his time. At issue was the tension between history – that is to say an awareness of temporality – and of life in the here and now. Nietzsche described the benefits, and in particular the dangers, represented by a concentration on historicity for his contemporaries in the realms of politics, ethics, and science. Today, of course, the question of the uses of architectural photography can hardly claim the same momentous status as Nietzsche's questioning of the relationship between past and present. But it does draw attention to the very definition of architecture and is hence relevant to anyone who is preoccupied with this theme.

To raise the question of whether architectural photography helps or hinders architecture already suggests that the relationship between the two is dynamic rather than static. My argument is that the relationship between architecture and photography shifts toward the center of interest when one or the other discipline – or both – finds itself in a state of change. In general, a consideration of the realm between art forms – between art and architecture, sculpture and painting, sculpture and performance – is fruitful as an indicator of a process of transformation. An investigation into the relationship between photography and architecture appears compelling because it brings to light processes that remain concealed when the histories of architecture and photography are examined separately.

The connection between photography and architecture extends all the way back to the 1830s, when photography was invented. It is a cliché that architecture is particularly well suited as a motif for photography because buildings do not move. It seems to me that this notion falls short since it is precisely those objects that are changeable and ephemeral that are attractive to photography. I believe the relationship between the then young medium of photography and architecture was intimate not so much because architecture was especially well suited to long exposure times (in that case, there should have been a particularly close relationship

Gebirgen bestehen –, sondern weil sich die Architektur damals vor den Augen der Menschen rapide veränderte. Einzelne Bauten, ja ganze Stadtteile wurden abgebrochen und mussten Platz für Neues machen. Die anhebende Industrialisierung transformierte die Umwelt in einer Weise, die die Zeitgenossen gleichermaßen faszinierte und verängstigte. Zwei zeitliche Systeme kollidierten. Und die Kamera, die zwar eine Maschine ist und damit ein Teil der Industrialisierung, aber auch eine Erweiterung der menschlichen Sinnesorgane und damit in einer vormodernen Tradition verhaftet, stand am Schnittpunkte dieser Spannung und registrierte diese Prozesse. Die Sympathie der Fotografen galt einer vergänglichen, zerbrechlichen Architektur, die wie die Menschen dem Lauf der Zeit unweigerlich unterworfen ist.

Die Transformation des Stadtbildes im Sog der Modernisierung ist das Thema, das sich wie ein roter Faden durch die Geschichte der Fotografie vom mittleren 19. Jahrhundert bis in die 1980er-Jahre zieht. Im Unterschied beispielsweise zum Porträt oder zur Landschaftsdarstellung ist dieses Genre, wenn man so will, der Fotografie eigen. Sie braucht sich an keine Konventionen der Bildenden Kunst anzulehnen. Und im Unterschied zu Diagrammen und Plänen, die Prozesse der urbanen Transformation auf eine abstrahierende und distanzierte Art darstellen, lässt die Fotografie die Betrachterinnen und Betrachter detailliert nachvollziehen, wie die Veränderung der gebauten Umwelt die Menschen verändert. Die vergilbten Abzüge und die undeutlichen Daguerreotypien aus dem 19. Jahrhundert rühren uns gerade deshalb im Rückblick als etwas Gegenwärtiges an – stärker als beispielsweise eine Grafik, ein Plan oder ein Gemälde –, weil wir uns mit den Menschen, deren Umgebung transformiert wird, identifizieren und deren Perspektive einnehmen können.

Ein prominentes Beispiel dafür ist eine der ersten Aufnahmen überhaupt, Louis Daguerres Daguerreotypie *Boulevard du Temple* (ca. 1838). Sie zeigt eine der damals beliebtesten Straßen in Paris, einen Treffpunkt der sozialen Klassen, die bald danach den Modernisierungen des Baron Haussmann und der damit einhergehenden Segregation in der Stadt, also der Trennung unterschiedlicher gesellschaftlichen Schichten, weichen sollte. **Abb. 1.** Bereits auf dieser Aufnahme wird ein grundsätzliches Problem der Fotografie erkennbar, nämlich die Schwierigkeit, die Menschen und ihre gebaute Umgebung auf derselben Darstellungsebene

between photography and mountains) but instead because at that time architecture was changing rapidly before people's eyes. Individual buildings, even entire urban districts, were being demolished to make space for the new. An advancing industrialization was transforming the environment in ways that were simultaneously fascinating and a source of anxiety. Two temporal systems collided. The camera – a machine and hence an aspect of industrialization, but also an extension of a human sensory organ and hence attached to a premodern tradition – stood at the intersection of the above tension and registered the process. Eliciting the sympathy of photographers was a transient, fragile architecture, one that was subject to the passage of time just like human beings.

The transformation of the cityscape in the wake of modernization is a recurrent theme and runs like a leitmotif through the history of photography from the mid-19th century until the 1980s. In contradistinction to the portrait or landscape, for example, the genre is, so to speak, intrinsic to photography. It need rely on none of the conventions of the fine arts. And unlike diagrams and design plans, which represent processes of urban transformation in an abstract and distanced fashion, photography allows the viewer to comprehend in a detailed way how the transformation of the built environment changes human beings. We find the yellowed photographic prints and indistinct daguerreotypes from the 19th century moving – more so, for example, than a print, a plan, or a painting – as something that seems to exist in the present moment because we identify with the people whose surroundings were being transformed and are able to adopt their perspective.

A prominent example of this is one of the first photographs ever made, Louis Daguerre's daguerreotype *Boulevard du Temple* (ca. 1838). It shows one of the then favorite streets in Paris, a meeting place for various social classes – a phenomenon that would vanish after Baron Haussmann's modernization and the urban segregation that accompanied it, that is to say the separation of the various social strata. Ill. 1. Evident already in this photograph is a fundamental problem with photography, namely the difficulty of registering people and their built surroundings on the same level of representation. As a consequence of the long exposure time, the street

festzuhalten. Aufgrund der langen Belichtungszeit wirkt die Straße leer. Alles, was in Bewegung ist, also Passanten, Tiere und Fahrzeuge, ist aus dem Bild verschwunden. Lediglich die Silhouetten eines Mannes und einer vor ihm knienden Person, möglicherweise ein Schuhputzer, sind bei genauem Hinsehen im Vordergrund zu erkennen. Angesichts der unscharfen Reproduktionen, die von der inzwischen weitgehend zerstörten Daguerrotypie existieren, lässt sich mit Genuss über diese leicht verschwommenen Staffagefiguren spekulieren. Hat Daguerre diese Menschen damals wahrgenommen? Hat er sie gar bewusst posieren lassen? Was immer die Antwort sein mag, die Aufnahme zeigt, dass die Apparatur an ihre Grenzen stößt, wenn es darum geht, Menschen und Umgebung gleichzeitig darzustellen.

Kann es sein, dass das optische beziehungsweise technische Problem, die Menschen und ihre gebaute Umgebung auf einer Repräsentationsebene abzubilden, auf einem theoretischen Problem beruht? Kann es sein, dass die von Karl Marx postulierte Entfremdung der Menschen von ihrer Arbeit und ihrer Umgebung als Folge der Industrialisierung in der Fotografie zu Tage tritt? Kann es sein, dass es der Apparatur selbst nicht möglich ist, diese durch die Industrialisierung geschaffene Kluft zu überbrücken und die Menschen und ihre Umgebung zu versöhnen? Ein Blick auf das Œuvre von Eugène Atget würde diese Hypothese bekräftigen. Atget dokumentierte während der urbanen Transformationsprozesse des ausgehenden 19. und frühen 20. Jahrhunderts die verwinkelten Gassen, die Hauseingänge und kleinen Plätze des teilweise noch durch mittelalterliche Strukturen geprägten Paris. Er nahm die Pariser Straßen und

1

appears empty. Everything in movement – passersby, animals, vehicles – has vanished from the image. Only the silhouette of a man and someone kneeling before him, possibly a shoeshine, are visible in the foreground upon closer inspection. Considering the blurry reproductions that exist of numerous daguerreotypes, so many of which have meanwhile been destroyed, there is pleasure to be had in speculating about these unfocused accessory figures. Did Daguerre notice them at the time? Did he perhaps even deliberately pose them? Regardless of what the truth may be, this image points up how the apparatus encounters its limits when it is a question of depicting people and their surroundings simultaneously.

Could it be that the optical or technical problem of depicting people and their built surroundings on the same representational level rests on a theoretical problem? Could it be that the alienation of people from their labor and their surroundings as a consequence of industrialization, as postulated by Karl Marx, becomes manifest in photography? Could it be that the apparatus itself is incapable of bridging this chasm, one engendered by industrialization, and reconciling human beings with their environment? A look at Eugène Atget's œuvre reinforces this hypothesis. During the urban processes of transformation that occurred during the late 19th and early 20th centuries, Atget documented the twisting alleyways, building entrances, and little squares of a Paris that was still characterized to some extent by medieval structures. III. 2. Almost always, he photographed the streets and squares of Paris empty of people. Walter Benjamin compared the photograph with the scene of a crime: "The scene of a crime, too, is deserted; it is photographed for the purpose of establishing evidence. With Atget, photographs become standard evidence for historical occurrences and acquire a hidden political significance. They demand a specific form of approach; free-floating contemplation is not appropriate to them. They stir the viewer; he feels challenged by then in a new way... For the first time, captions have become obligatory."[1]

What Atget could not show in these crime scenes were the perpetrators, the driving forces of urban transformation. But can capitalism be depicted at all? Again, it is architectural photography that discovers a

Plätze fast immer menschenleer auf. Abb. 2. Walter Benjamin verglich die Fotografien mit Aufnahmen eines Tatorts: „Auch der Tatort ist menschenleer. Seine Aufnahme erfolgt der Indizien wegen. Die photographischen Aufnahmen beginnen bei Atget, Beweisstücke im historischen Prozess zu werden. Das macht ihre verborgene politische Bedeutung aus. Sie fordern schon eine Rezeption in bestimmtem Sinne. Ihnen ist die freischwebende Kontemplation nicht mehr angemessen. Sie beunruhigen den Betrachter; er fühlt: zu ihnen muss er einen bestimmten Weg suchen. [...] In ihnen ist die Beschriftung zum ersten Mal obligat geworden."[1]

Was Atget in diesen Tatorten nicht zeigen konnte, waren die Täter beziehungsweise die treibenden Kräfte der urbanen Transformation. Wie aber lässt sich der Kapitalismus überhaupt darstellen? Wieder ist es die Architekturfotografie, die dafür eine Form findet, in Gestalt von Paul Strands Aufnahme *Wall Street* (1915). Abb. 3. Die Aufnahme zeigt die Fassade des 1913 eröffneten Hauptsitzes der J.P. Morgan Bank in New York. Niemand, der das Bild gesehen hat, wird die kleinen, ameisenartigen Figuren vergessen, die zur morgendlichen Rushhour an den riesigen schwarzen Fassadenöffnungen vorbeieilen. Strand selbst sagte im Rückblick: „Well, I also was fascinated by all these little people walking by these great big sinister, almost threatening shapes... these black, repetitive, rectangular shapes – sort of blind shapes, because you can't see in, with people going by."[2] Strand sagte „blind shapes". In Wirklichkeit handelt es sich um Nischen, in die Fenster eingelassen sind. Die mysteriösen Nischen rahmen und ordnen die vorbeiziehenden Angestellten, sie stehen für die Autorität der Bank, aber auch für die Segmentierung von Raum und Zeit, für Repetition und Akkumulation und für Abstraktion als Prinzipien der Industrialisierung und des modernen Kapitalismus. Sie zwingen den Individuen den Rhythmus auf und vereinzeln diese zugleich im Sinne der Arbeitsteilung. Sie strukturieren die Fotografie wie Perforationslöcher einen Film und unterstreichen damit den Eindruck der Wiederholung; sie erinnern an die industrielle Struktur nicht nur der Fließbandarbeit der Arbeiterinnen und Arbeiter, sondern auch der Arbeit der Angestellten in ihren Büros und Verwaltungen. Und sie bewirken, dass die Struktur der Fotografie und die Fotografie der architektonischen Struktur ineinander übergehen und sich nicht mehr klar voneinander trennen lassen. Es scheint, als wäre die harte, glatte Oberfläche des Granits, dessen Textur

form capable of doing so, specifically in Paul Strand's photograph *Wall Street* (1915). Ill. 3. The image shows the facade of the headquarters of the J.P. Morgan Bank in New York, inaugurated in 1913. No one who has seen this picture will ever forget the tiny, antlike figures who hurry past the gigantic black apertures in the early morning rush hour. Strand himself said in retrospect, "Well, I also was fascinated by all these little people walking by these great big sinister, almost threatening shapes ... these black, repetitive, rectangular shapes – sort of blind shapes, because you can't see in, with people going by."[2] Strand refers to "blind shapes." In reality, they are niches into which windows have been set. The mysterious niches both frame and order the passing office workers and stand for the bank's authority but also for the segmentation of space and time, for repetition, accumulation, and abstraction as principles of industrialization and modern capitalism. They impose a rhythm upon the individual and at the same time particularize him or her in the spirit of the division of labor. They structure the photograph like film perforations, thereby underscoring the impression of iteration; in their industrial structure, they recall not only the assembly line work performed by modern laborers but also the duties performed by white-collar workers in their offices and administrative departments. And they effect a merging between the structure of the photograph and the architectural structure, which can no longer be clearly differentiated from one another. It seems as though the hard, smooth surface of the granite, its

2

durch das helle Morgenlicht hervorgehoben wird, in der fein gekörnten Oberfläche des quecksilberbeschichteten Platinabzugs enthalten, der ja ebenfalls durch den Abdruck von Licht auf einer lichtempfindlichen Emulsion zustande kommt. Die Architektur ist zur Fotografie transformiert, die sich seinerseits der kollektiven Imagination einprägte.

Während Strands Aufnahme die Architektur in einem Bild komprimiert, erstellte Margaret Bourke-White, vergleichbar mit Atget, Bildserien. Sie begleitete in den ausgehenden 1920er- und frühen 1930er-Jahren den Aufbau der Schwerindustrie in den USA und in der Sowjetunion. Ihre Aufnahmen vom Bau von Magnitogorsk schärften den Blick der Zeitgenossen für die erhabene Schönheit der Industriearchitektur und stehen exemplarisch für den Fortschrittsglauben jener Jahre. Dabei verlor sie nie die Menschen aus den Augen und wechselte vom Maßstab der Hochöfen und Großbaustellen zum Maßstab der einzelnen Arbeiterinnen und Arbeiter, ohne die diese Bauten nicht hätten entstehen können. Als der Mittlere Westen der USA, die „Dust Bowl", in den 1930er-Jahren von einer Dürrekatastrophe heimgesucht wird, zeigt sie mit ihren Aufnahmen, wie die gebaute Umgebung sich gegen die Bewohner richtet. Die Behausungen spenden keinen Schutz mehr, sondern werden zu Gefängnissen. Die Straßen bieten keine Perspektive mehr, sondern werden zu Orten der Hoffnungslosigkeit. Zur selben Zeit unternahm Walker Evans im Auftrag der amerikanischen Behörden eine Expedition in die von der Rezession gebeutelten amerikanischen Südstaaten und zeichnete die verheerende Wirkung der Arbeitslosigkeit auf seine Zeitgenossen auf. Zu den eindrücklichsten Aufnahmen gehören seine Bilder der von Afro-Amerikanern bewohnten Stadtteile im Bundesstaat Mississippi. Eine der Aufnahmen zeigt ein Friseurgeschäft, vor dem drei Männer warten und in die Kamera blicken. Unter dem Druck der Krise wurde es für die Kamera möglich, die Menschen und die Straße gleichzeitig darzustellen. Aber gerade dadurch, dass wir Gruppen von Menschen in erwerbsfähigem Alter am helllichten Tage vor ihren Häusern sehen, erfahren wir, dass sie keine Arbeit haben und die ökonomische und gesellschaftliche Ordnung zerrüttet ist. Die Misere, die Ausweglosigkeit wird durch die Bretterfassaden symbolisiert, die den Bildraum gleichsam verriegeln. Der Stadtraum ist kein Ort der Bewegung mehr; die Straße führt nirgendwohin, sie ist zur trostlosen Bühne der Stagnation geworden.

texture accentuated by the pale morning light, is present in the finely grained surface of the mercury-coated platinum print, itself likewise formed by light falling on a photosensitive emulsion. Architecture is transmuted into photography, which for its part conditions the collective imagination.

While Strand's photograph compresses architecture into an image, Margaret Bourke-White produced series of images in ways comparable to Atget. In the late 1920s and early 1930s, she observed the buildup of heavy industry in the US and the Soviet Union. Her photographs of the construction of Magnitogorsk sensitized the eyes of her contemporaries to the sublime beauty of industrial architecture, and they exemplify the faith in progress that characterized those years. At the same time they never lose sight of the human dimension and shift from the scale of blast furnaces and construction sites to that of the individual worker – without whom the structures could not have existed. When the Midwestern US, what had become the 'Dust Bowl', was plagued in the 1930s by catastrophic drought, her images showed how the built environment could turn against its inhabitants. Dwellings no longer provided shelter and were transformed into prisons instead. Streets no longer offered any perspective, instead becoming places of hopelessness. At the same time Walker Evans accepted a commission from the American authorities to make a tour of the recession-stricken American southern states in order to depict the devastating impact of joblessness on his contemporaries. Among his most striking images are photographs of African-American neighborhoods in the state of Mississippi. One shows a barbershop with three men waiting out front, gazing into the camera.

3

Die Architekturfotografie als spezialisierte Gattung prosperierte während des Wirtschaftsbooms der Nachkriegszeit. Allerdings stand sie weitgehend im Dienst der Architektur und vermittelte diese möglichst effektvoll. Ende der 1980er-Jahre war sie derart konventionell geworden, dass sie sich als Gattung zu erschöpfen begann. Impulse kamen in erster Linie von der bildenden Kunst, zu der die Fotografie inzwischen zählte. Künstlerinnen und Künstler wie Candida Höfer und Thomas Struth zeigten, wie aus künstlerischer Perspektive ein neuer Blick auf die Architektur möglich wurde. Der katalanische Architekt und Theoretiker Ignasi Solà-Morales Rubió stellte 1995 in seinem Essay „Terrain vague" fest, dass die moderne Metropole sich nicht mehr adäquat durch die Abbildung einer Skyline oder einzelner Bauten darstellen ließe. Einen viel besseren Eindruck böten Aufnahmen von Industriebrachen und unbenutzten Zonen, die in den 1980er- und frühen 1990er-Jahren Fotografen wie John Davies, Manolo Laguillo, und Jannes Linders gemacht hatten.[3] Solà-Morales erkannte das Potenzial des Begriffs „terrain vague", der nicht fixiert sei und gleichermaßen positiv wie negativ konnotiert verwendet werden könne. In seinen Worten evozierte er „Leere, Abwesenheit, aber auch Versprechen, den Raum des Möglichen, der Erwartung."[4]

Im Rückblick können wir nachvollziehen, warum er als Architekt das terrain vague als Versprechen auffasste und warum er der Ansicht war, die Zeitgenossen haben im Konflikt mit sich selbst gestanden. Während der Boom-Jahre der 1980er und frühen 1990er war ganz Europa eine Baustelle. Städte wie Paris, London, Berlin und Barcelona erholten sich von der Deindustrialisierung und der Rezession der 1970er-Jahre. Die Transformation deindustrialisierter Zonen wie des parc de la Villette in Paris, der Docklands in London, des Potsdamer Platzes in Berlin, und des Parque de Diagonal Mar in Barcelona war ein Schlüsselthema der architektonischen Debatte. Es war ein Eldorado für Architektinnen und Architekten; die leeren Flächen waren wie Goldminen, voller ästhetischer und wirtschaftlicher Versprechen. Im Zug der Wettbewerbe, die damals ausgelobt wurden, begriffen die Architektinnen und Architekten, dass sie hier möglicherweise zum letzten Mal die Möglichkeit hatten, die Form der Großstadt mitzuprägen und zu verhindern, dass diese ganz in die Hände von Investoren fiele. Und abermals gab es kein Medium, das diese Dynamik so gut ins Bild setzen konnte wie die Fotografie.

Under the pressure of the crisis, it became possible for the camera to show people and streets simultaneously. And precisely because we see groups of working-age people standing in front of their homes in the light of day, we realize that they have no work, that the economic and social order has become unhinged. Their misery and hopelessness is symbolized by the facades, composed of thin boards, which at the same time block off the picture space. The urban space is no longer a place of movement; the streets lead nowhere, have become a desolate setting for stagnation.

As a specialized genre, architectural photography prospered during the economic boom of the postwar era. For the most part, indeed, it stood in the service of architecture, which it conveyed with maximum effectiveness. By the late 1980s, it had become so conventionalized that its growing exhaustion as a genre was now apparent. Fresh impulses arrived mainly from the realm of the fine arts, where photography had meanwhile fully arrived. Artists such as Candida Höfer and Thomas Struth demonstrated how an artistic perspective could offer new vantage points on architecture. In 1995, the Catalan architect and theoretician Ignasi Solà-Morales Rubió pointed out in the essay "Terrain vague" that the modern metropolis could no longer be represented adequately by depictions of skylines or individual buildings. According to him, a far better impression was offered by the images of industrial wastelands and disused zones, as depicted in the 1980s and early 1990s by photographers such as John Davies, Manolo Laguillo, and Jannes Linders.[3] Solà-Morales recognized the potential of the term terrain vague, whose meaning was not fixed and could be connoted simultaneously as positive or negative. In his words, it evoked "void, absence, yet also promise, the space of the possible, of expectation."[4]

In retrospect, it becomes comprehensible why, as an architect, he invoked the potential of the terrain vague, and why he took the view that his contemporaries were in conflict with themselves. During the boom years of the 1980s and early 1990s, all of Europe was a building site. Cities such as Paris, London, Berlin, and Barcelona began to recover from the deindustrialization and recession of the 1970s. The transformation of deindustrialized zones such as the Parc de la Villette in Paris, the Docklands in London, Potsdamer Platz in

Die eindrücklichen Aufnahmen von Industriebrachen und Baustellen, die beispielsweise Bernd und Hilla Becher, Eveline Richter, Aglaia Konrad Abb. 4 und Lara Almarcegui schufen, haben die Vorstellungen einer ganzen Generation von Architektinnen und Architekten geprägt. Sie stehen allerdings auch am Ende einer langen fotografischen Tradition. Manche Theoretikerinnen und Theoretiker begründen dies mit dem Wechsel von der analogen zur digitalen Technik. Natürlich dürfen wir die Veränderung der Apparatur nicht unterschätzen, aber ich würde sie weniger stark gewichten als die tief greifende Veränderung der Vorstellung von Zeit, die in derselben Zeit stattfand. Wenn Theoretiker wie Michael Hardt und Antoni Negri zu Recht behaupten, dass wir uns auf eine historische Phase zu bewegen, in der die zeitlichen und räumlichen Grenzen aufgehoben werden und in einer „geglätteten Welt" das zeitliche Nacheinander durch das räumliche Nebeneinander abgelöst, ja die Zeit zum Stillstand kommen wird, dann bedeutet dies für die Fotografie eine Herausforderung.[5] Wenn der Lauf der Zeit derart gebremst wird, dass die Zeit quasi still steht und eine Art ewige Gegenwart entsteht, dann muss sich die Kamera neu orientieren. Es kann nicht mehr ihr Verdienst sein, Momente festzuhalten, die sonst unwiederbringlich verloren wären. Es kann nicht mehr ihre Aufgabe sein, sich gegen den Lauf der Zeit zu stemmen. Vielmehr muss sie Orientierung in einer Räumlichkeit geben, die keine Anhaltspunkte mehr bietet.

Nachdem die Kunst der Kamera anderthalb Jahrhunderte lang darin bestand, möglichst still zu stehen, um die Bewegung einfangen zu können, muss sie heute möglichst beweglich sein, um den Stillstand einfangen

4

Berlin, and the Parque de Diagonal Mar in Barcelona became a key topic of architectural debate. Here was an El Dorado for architects, the empty surfaces like gold-mines, filled with aesthetic and economic potential. In the course of the competitions that were announced at the time, architects realized that this might be their last opportunity to contribute to shaping large cities and to prevent them from falling entirely into the hands of investors. And once again, no other medium was capable of visualizing this dynamic like photography.

The striking photographs of industrial wastelands and building sites created by Bernd and Hilla Becher, Eveline Richter, Aglaia Konrad, III.4, and Lara Almarcegui, for example, have shaped the imaginations of an entire generation of architects. These artists stand, however, at the end of a long photographic tradition. Some theoreticians explain this in terms of the transition from analog to digital technology. Of course we can hardly underestimate the importance of such changes to the apparatus, but I regard them as less decisive than the profound transformation in our conception of time that took place during the same period. When theoreticians such as Michael Hardt and Antoni Negri assert correctly that we move within a historical phase in which temporal and spatial boundaries have been suspended, a "smooth world" where temporal succession has been supplanted by spatial juxtaposition and time has come to a standstill, then this represents a challenge for photography.[5] When the progress of time is arrested in such a way that time, so to speak, stands still and a kind of eternal present emerges, then the camera must reorient itself. Its virtue is no longer a capacity to capture moments that would otherwise be irretrievably lost. Its task is no longer to check the forward flow of time. Instead, it must provide orientation within a spatial order that no longer provides reliable points of reference.

Today, after a century and a half during which the art of the camera was to remain as motionless as possible in order to capture movement, it must remain maximally mobile in order to capture the cessation of movement. This has led to the circumstance that video represents its greatest competitor or, alternatively, the very horizon of photographic practice. Photographs of architecture and urban planning, therefore, must continuously register virtually everything. What counts

zu können. Dies hat dazu geführt, dass das Video zu ihrer größten Konkurrenz beziehungsweise zum Horizont der fotografischen Praxis wurde. Fotografen von Architektur und Städtebau müssen deshalb quasi fortwährend alles registrieren. Nicht die optimale Beleuchtung des einzelnen Gebäudes zählt, sondern das Gespür für die Bewegungen des Terrains der gebauten Umwelt. So gesehen, wird beispielsweise die Errichtung von Infrastrukturbauten in China, die um die Jahrtausendwende fast die gesamte Stahlproduktion der Welt absorbierten, zu einem Faktor, der noch auf die unscheinbarste Baustelle in Österreich Auswirkungen hat – zum Beispiel in Bezug auf die Materialkosten –, die aber wiederum niemand so deutlich zeigen kann wie die Fotografen. Fotografinnen und Fotografen wie Armin Linke **Abb. 5**, Simona Rota **Abb. 6** und Anne Lass gehören zu den Protagonisten in diesem Bereich. Obwohl keine klassische Architekturfotografie, haben die Aufnahmen von den Brennpunkten der globalisierten Ökonomie dazu beigetragen, dass sich das Bild dessen, was Architektur ist und wie sie mit den Veränderungen im globalem Maßstab zusammenhängt, heute differenzierter darstellt als vor zwanzig oder dreißig Jahren. Diese Aufnahmen beschränken sich nicht auf die Darstellung der fertigen Bauten, sondern beziehen das Gewinnen von Bodenschätzen, die Wege des Transports, die Unterbringung von Bauarbeitern, aber auch den raschen Zerfall der Bauten, sobald das Kapital abzieht, mit ein. Die Gegenstände der Architekturfotografie, so können wir von Fotografinnen und Fotografen wie Rota, Lass und Linke lernen, geht weit über Gebäude und Stadtansichten hinaus.

now is not the optimal illumination of individual buildings but instead a feel for the movements that occur in the terrain of the built environment. Viewed in this way, the construction of infrastructural buildings in China, for example, which around the turn-of-the-century absorbed nearly the world's entire steel production, becomes a factor that impacts the most inconspicuous building site in Austria (with regard to material costs, for example), but which, again, no one else is able to expose so clearly as the photographer. Among the protagonists in this area are Armin Linke III. 5, Simona Rota III. 6 and Anne Lass. Although not regarded as classical architectural photography, these images of the hot spots of the globalized economy contribute to a more differentiated picture than 20 or 30 years ago of what architecture is and how it is related to transformations occurring on a global scale. These photographs are not restricted to images of completed buildings, but also incorporate the extraction of mineral resources, transport routes, the accommodations of construction workers, and the rapid disintegration of buildings as soon as capital withdraws. As we learn from the work of photographers like Rota, Lass, and Linke, the subjects of architectural photography go far beyond buildings and cityscapes.

What challenges does architectural photography face today? Which phenomena is it uniquely capable of visualizing? Of course the documentation of buildings and urban districts is indispensable when it comes to making them known to a broader public. Architectural criticism and architectural history – along with teaching and research – would remain inconceivable without architectural photography. Just as art can hardly

5

Welches sind heute die Herausforderungen für die Architekturfotografie? Welches sind Phänomene, die nur sie sichtbar machen kann? Natürlich ist die Dokumentation von Bauten und Stadtteilen unverzichtbar, wenn es darum geht, sie einer weiten Öffentlichkeit bekannt zu machen. Ohne Architekturfotografie wären weder die Architekturkritik noch die Architekturgeschichte noch die Lehre und Forschung denkbar. So, wie die Kunst auf die Ausstellung unmöglich verzichten kann, bliebe auch die Wirkung von Architektur ohne Fotografie sehr begrenzt. Aber mir geht es nicht primär um diese unterstützende Funktion der Fotografie im Sinne der Verbreitung beziehungsweise Propaganda. Wichtiger scheint mir das Potenzial von Fotografie als Instrument der kritischen Analyse. Sie kann den Architektinnen und Architekten einen Spiegel vorhalten, der ihnen nicht nur das eigene Tun in helleres Licht rückt, sondern auch buchstäblich den Horizont erweitert, indem sie zeigt, was war, was kommen könnte und was möglich wäre.

renounce the public exhibition, the impact of architecture without photography would be limited. But I am not concerned primarily with this supportive function, i.e., with dissemination and propaganda. More crucial, it seems to me, is the potential of photography as an instrument of critical analysis. It can hold up a mirror to architects – not only situating their own achievements in a clearer light but also literally expanding their horizons by showing them what was, what might come about, what might become possible.

6

1 Walter Benjamin, „Das Kunstwerk im Zeitalter seiner technischen Reproduzierbarkeit" in: Walter Benjamin, *Gesammelte Schriften*, hg. von Rolf Tiedemann und Hermann Schweppenhäuser, Bd. I, 2, Suhrkamp, Frankfurt a. M., 1980, S. 471 – 508, hier: S. 485.
2 Paul Strand, zitiert nach: Maria Morris Hambourg, „Introduction", in: *Paul Strand, Circa 1916*, The Metropolitan Museum of Art, New York, Abrams, 1998, S. 28 – 29.
3 Ignasi de Solà-Morales Rubió, „Terrain vague", in: *Anyplace*, MIT Press, Cambridge, Mass., 1995, S. 118 – 123.
4 Ebd., S. 120 (Übersetzung Philip Ursprung).
5 Michael Hardt, Antonio Negri: *Empire. Die neue Weltordnung*. Aus dem Englischen von Thomas Atzert und Andreas Wirthensohn. Campus Verlag, Frankfurt a. M. 2002, S. 11. (Empire, Cambridge, Mass., 2000).

1 Walter Benjamin, "The Work of Art in the Age of Mechanical Reproduction," in: *Illuminations*, Hannah Arendt (ed.), Harcourt, Brace & World, New York, 1968, p. 226.
2 Paul Strand, cited by Maria Morris Hambourg, "Introduction," in: *Paul Strand, Circa 1916*, New York: Metropolitan Museum of Art, Abrams, 1998, pp. 28 – 29.
3 Ignasi de Solà-Morales Rubió, "Terrain vague," in: *Anyplace*, MIT Press, Cambridge, Mass., 1995, pp. 118 – 123.
4 Ibid., p. 120.
5 Michael Hardt, Antonio Negri, *Empire*, Harvard University Press, Cambridge, Mass., 2000.

Von der Nutzung der
Architektur in der Fotografie
On the Uses of Architecture
in Photography

Elke Krasny

Am Anfang wie am Ende dieses Essays steht jeweils ein Gebäude, das nicht mehr existiert. Es ist kaum zu erwarten, dass man diesen Gebäuden je in einem konventionellen Stadtführer oder in einer herkömmlichen Architekturgeschichte begegnen wird können. Sie werden der Aufmerksamkeit entgangen sein. Für die Präzisierung einer kritischen Befragung der Verhältnisse zwischen Architektur, Nutzung und Fotografie sind diese beiden Gebäude, wie ich zeigen werde, jedoch durchaus von entscheidender Bedeutung. Das eine der beiden Gebäude befand sich in Hamburg, das andere in Belgrad. Das erste lernte ich durch wiederholte Besuche immer wieder von neuen Seiten kennen. Das zweite kenne ich aus Gesprächen mit der Künstlerin, in deren Arbeit das Gebäude eine zentrale Rolle spielt, und durch die dokumentarischen Fotografien ihrer installativen Arbeit gezeigt wurden. Die Nutzungen dieser beiden Gebäude – im ersten Fall handelt es sich um eine Restnutzung bis zum Abriss, im zweiten Fall um ein Nachleben nach dem Abriss – bilden den Eingang in sowie den Ausgang aus diesem Essay. Der zentrale Raum in der Mitte, in den sie hinein- und aus dem sie wieder herausführen, ist mit der Beschreibung und Analyse einer fotografischen Schlüsselszene befasst, die von der Darstellung der Architektur der Moderne handelt. Die Architektur, von der hier die Rede sein wird, hat einen fixen Platz in der Geschichte der Architektur eingenommen. Anhand der Rolle der Fotografie in der Darstellung und Überlieferungstradition dieser Architektur wird sich deren diskursive Formierung offen legen lassen. Der Schlüssel zur Bedeutung dieser Schlüsselszene liegt, wie ich aufzeigen werde, in der Rolle, die die Architekturfotografie dabei spielt, den Diskurs der Architektur der Moderne zu formieren.

Ich möchte nun mit dem Gebäude in Hamburg beginnen. Dieses befand sich im Stadtteil Wilhelmsburg im Reihersteigviertel am Rotenhäuser Feld auf dem Areal des ehemaligen Gesundheitsamts und war seit über zehn Jahren nicht mehr genutzt worden. Für diesen brachliegenden, bereits im Verfall befindlichen Bau wurde im Jahr 2007 auf Initiative der Internationalen Bauausstellung (IBA) an der HafenCity Universität (HCU) ein studentischer Ideenwettbewerb ausgeschrieben. 2007 waren die Vorbereitungsarbeiten für die IBA, die 2013 stattfinden sollte, bereits in Gang. Die IBA setzte zum „Sprung über die Elbe" auf die größte Flussinsel Europas in dem migrantisch geprägten Stadtteil Wilhelmsburg an.[1]

At the beginning and the end of this essay respectively stands a building that no longer exists. One can hardly expect to encounter these buildings in ordinary city guides or conventional histories of architecture. They easily escape attention. For a critical interrogation of the relationship between architecture, use, and photography, both of the buildings I want to present are nonetheless of decisive importance. One is found in Hamburg, the other in Belgrade. Through repeated visits I have become acquainted with new aspects of the first building over and over again. The second is known to me through conversations with an artist in whose work the building plays a central role and through documentary photographs of her installation. The uses of these two buildings – for the first, it is a question of a residual use that continued until it was razed; in the second case, of an afterlife following demolition – form the entry point and conclusion of my essay. The central section, into and out of which these episodes lead, describes and analyzes a key photographic scene, one that involves the depiction of architecture of the modern. The architecture under discussion has come to occupy a fixed position within architectural history. Through a reference to the role of photography in the tradition of representing and transmitting this architecture, its discursive formation is revealed. As I will show, the key to the meaning of the key scene lies in the role performed by architectural photography in shaping the discourse on the architecture of modernism.

I will now proceed with the building in Hamburg. It is located in the Wilhelmsburg district on Rotenhäuser Feld in the Reihersteig quarter on the premises of the former Gesundheitsamt (public health department) and was left disused for more than ten years. In 2007, on the initiative of the Internationale Bauausstellung (IBA) at HafenCity University (HCU), a student ideas competition was announced for this building, which was lying fallow and already in a state of deterioration. In 2007, preparations were already in progress for the IBA, scheduled to be held in 2013. The IBA launched "Leap across the Elbe" on Europe's largest river island in the urban district of Wilhelmsburg, whose character is shaped by an immigrant community.[1] The site on Rotenhäuser Feld would be a part of the IBA: "As a temporary building complex (which will remain until the final presentation

Der Standort am Rotenhäuser Feld sollte Teil der IBA werden: „Diese Fläche soll als temporär angelegter Baukomplex – bis zur Endpräsentation der IBA im Jahre 2013 – Raum bieten für eine aktive Kooperation zwischen der IBA, der HCU, der Kulturfabrik Kampnagel und den Menschen im Stadtteil sowie weiteren Gästen, die gemeinsam an der Entwicklung der Elbinsel mitwirken wollen."[2] Insgesamt nahmen 65 Studierende aus den Departments Architektur, Bauingenieurwesen und Stadtplanung in interdisziplinären Teams an dem Wettbewerb teil.[3] Interessanterweise hatten neun der zehn eingereichten Wettbewerbsbeiträge den Vorschlag gemacht, das Bestandsgebäude komplett abzureißen und durch den Neubau von Pavillons zu ersetzen. Das Experimentelle oder das Innovative hätte von der Form getragen und geleistet werden müssen. Nur der Wettbewerbssieger votierte für den Erhalt des Bestands. Unter dem Titel „Grenzposten" schlugen Anton Reinig, Carsten Dittus, Kate Bitz, Maximilian Müller und Nicole Raddatz „Betrieb und Nutzung" vor; unter anderem dachten sie dabei an ein HCU-Graduiertenkolleg, an eine Flüchtlingsanlaufstelle, an Oral-History-Abende oder an eine Open University.[4] Das Entscheidende für das Experiment einer Neuorientierung lag nicht in einem formalen Vorschlag begründet, sondern in einer Definition des Orts durch eine Vielfalt von Nutzungen.

Das Ergebnis des Wettbewerbs legte den konzeptuellen Grundstein für die Restzukunft des Gebäudes. Unter der Leitung von Bernd Kniess, Professor für Städtebau/Urban Design an der HCU, wurde die Universität als Nachbarschaftsprojekt mit lokalen und translokalen Bezügen von Benjamin Becker, Stefanie Gernert und Michael Koch entwickelt. Zwischen 2008 und 2013 beherbergte das Bestandsgebäude einschließlich des ihn umgebenden Gartens das temporäre Projekt der Restnutzung. Die Universitätsgründung begann als Umbau, die Institutionswerdung vollzog sich als Rückbau – beides bei zeitgleicher Erprobung von Nutzungen. Das experimentelle Curriculum, Lehre und Forschung, bildete das inhaltliche Gerüst für die Restnutzung. Alle Beteiligten wussten, dass am Ende dieses Experiments einer Universität auf Zeit definitiv der Abriss des Bestandsgebäudes stehen würde. Aus dem Wissen um die begrenzte Zeit bezog das Projekt seine Energie. Während viele der neuen Projekte der IBA auf Vorzeigebauten einer neuen „Smart City" Wilhelmsburg setzten,[5] handelt es sich bei der Universität der Nachbarschaft um eine

in 2013), the premises will offer a space for active cooperation between the International Building Exhibition Hamburg (IBA), HafenCity University Hamburg (HCU), the Kulturfabrik Kampnagel, and local residents, as well as visitors who wish to contribute to developments on Elbe Island."[2] Participating in the competition in interdisciplinary teams were 65 students in all from the Departments of Architecture, Engineering, and City Planning.[3] Interestingly, nine of the ten competition entries that were submitted proposed completely demolishing the existing building and replacing it with a newly constructed pavilion. The experimental and the innovative were to have been supported and accomplished via form alone. Only the competition winner opted for preserv-ing the building. Under the title "Grenzposten" (border posts), Anton Reinig, Carsten Dittus, Kate Bitz, Maximilian Müller, and Nicole Raddatz proposed a program for "operations and uses"; among other things, they envisioned a HCU research training group, a drop-in-center for refugees, an oral history evening, and an open university.[4] The decisive aspect of this experimental reorientation was not a formal proposal but instead the redefinition of a place in terms of a plurality of uses.

The competition results laid the conceptual cornerstone for the remainder of the building's future. Under the direction of Bernd Kniess, Professor for Städtebau/Urban Design at the HCU, the university was developed by Benjamin Becker, Stefanie Gernert, and Michael Koch as a neighborhood project with local and translocal points of reference. Between 2008 and 2013, the existing building together with the surrounding garden accommodated the temporary residual-use project. The founding of the university began as a conversion, and its institutional development was implemented through a demolition; both of these proceeded through the concurrent testing of different uses. The experimental curriculum, teaching, and research program formed the scaffolding in terms of content for the residual use. All participants knew that at the end of the experiment the existing building housing the temporary university faced demolition. The project drew its dynamism from this awareness of its limited time span. While many new IBA projects rely upon the flagship buildings of a new "Smart City" of Wilhelmsburg[5], this University of Neighborhoods was concerned with a process of transformation

and was implemented in a time-limited fashion through intensive (re)use. The team, together with Bernd Kniess, spoke of an "architecture of possibility for a learning city".[6] Formats such as the Wilhelmsburg Orchestra III.1, initiated by Christopher Dell, the Kitchen Salon and the Hotel Wilhelmsburg were occupied and tested out at this location.

Analyzing the photographs and descriptions that document the "Neighborhood University," I arrive at the conclusion that the building receded behind its uses. It retreated almost completely into the background, becoming to some extent invisible. The structure revealed itself as a material foundation of possibilities for a multiplicity of activities. As I argue below, this points to the circumstance that the building was situated "beyond the profit maximization of the real estate industry", and could therefore be tested through experimental uses; it did not have to be foregrounded in visual terms. Here, architectural photography shifts to the margin of the constructed in order to display the activities the building made possible, those which were attached to it and intervened in it.[7] Utilization emerges now into the foreground. This is indicated by the activities taking place in and around the built structures and by their traces, whose use value is documented photographically. The space was found in a continuous state of residual use. The political dimension manifested in this residual use, not least of all through photography, can be examined with Michel de Certeau from the perspective of the political philosophy of everyday life, and with Judith Butler from a materialist-feminist perspective. "In short, space is a practiced place."[8] The existing building, the place, was converted into the space of the University of Neighborhoods. III.2, In her 2012 article "Bodies in Alliance and the Politics of the Street" Judith Butler argues that politics is always an intersection between private and public: "At such a moment, politics is not defined as taking place exclusively in the public sphere distinct from a private one, but it crosses those lines again and again, bringing attention to the way that politics is already in the home or on the street or in the neighborhood…"[9] Butler continues by arguing that the existing material surroundings are actively reconfigured and defamiliarized at the moment when political protest goes out into the street. Turning away from questions of protest or strikes, she

transformative Veränderung, die in zeitlicher Begrenzung durch intensive (Um-)Nutzung stattfindet. Das Team um Bernd Kniess spricht von einer „Ermöglichungsarchitektur für die lernende Stadt."[6] Formate wie das von Christopher Dell initiierte Wilhelmsburg Orchestra Abb.1, der Küchen-Salon und das Hotel Wilhelmsburg bespielten und erprobten den Ort.

Analysiere ich die Fotografien und Beschreibungen, die die Universität der Nachbarschaften dokumentieren, so gelange ich zu folgendem Ergebnis: Das Gebäude tritt hinter den Nutzungen zurück. Es tritt fast vollständig in den Hintergrund, wird teilweise nahezu unsichtbar. Das Gebäude erweist sich als materielle Ermöglichungsgrundlage für eine Vielzahl von Handlungen. Wie ich weiterführend argumentieren möchte, verweist dies ursächlich auf den Umstand, dass dieses Gebäude sich im „Abseits des immobilienwirtschaftlichen Verwertungszusammenhangs" befand, deshalb in experimentellen Nutzungen erprobt werden und visuell nicht in den Vordergrund treten musste. Die Architekturfotografie gerät hier an den äußeren Rand des Gebauten und zeigt die Handlungen, die durch das Gebaute ermöglicht werden, sich daran anlagern und darin eingreifen.[7] Die Nutzungen treten in den Vordergrund. Dies zeigt sich in den Handlungen und deren Gebrauchsspuren am und im Gebauten, dessen Gebrauchswert sich in den dokumentarischen fotografischen Aufnahmen zeigt. Der Raum befand sich in einer dauerhaften Restnutzung. Die politische Dimension, die sich – nicht zuletzt durch die Fotografien – in dieser Restnutzung manifestiert, lässt sich sowohl mit Michel de Certeau aus der Perspektive der politischen Philosophie des Alltags als auch mit Judith Butler aus einer materialistisch-feministischen Perspektive betrachten. „Insgesamt

1

ist der Raum ein Ort, mit dem man etwas macht."[8] Das Bestandsgebäude, der Ort, wurde zum Raum der Universität der Nachbarschaften Abb. 2 gemacht. In ihrem 2012 erschienenen Artikel "Bodies in Alliance and the Politics of the Street" argumentiert Judith Butler zum einen damit, dass Politik immer schon das Private und das Öffentliche gekreuzt und gequert habe und nicht nur in der Sphäre des Öffentlichen anzusiedeln sei: "At such a moment, politics is not defined as taking place exclusively in the public sphere distinct from a private one, but it crosses those lines again and again, bringing attention to the way that politics is already in the home, or on the street, or in the neighborhood (…)."[9] Butler setzt ihre Argumentation damit fort, dass die bestehende materielle Umgebung im Moment des politischen Protests, der auf die Straße geht, aktiv rekonfiguriert und verfremdet werde. Sie folgert daraus, den Moment des Protests oder Streiks verlassend, dass jede menschliche Handlung von Unterstützung, vom materiellen Unterstütztsein, abhängig sei:[10] „Human action depends upon all sorts of supports – it is always supported action."[11] Entsteht der Raum durch den Ort, mit dem gehandelt wird, so ist der Raum die materielle Umgebung, die physische Grundlage, die das Handeln unterstützt. Die Vielfalt der Nutzungen, die Experimente, Soziabilität und Konvivialität bedürfen der Unterstützung durch das Gebaute. Im Fall der Universität der Nachbarschaften war es ein bereits dem Verfall preisgegebenes, leer stehendes Gebäude, das nochmals aufgebaut, umgebaut und hergerichtet wurde, um dem Handeln Unterstützung zu bieten und dadurch zum Raum zu werden. Die fotografischen Aufnahmen der Universität der Nachbarschaft bezeugen den Wert der Nutzung.

2

concludes that every human action is dependent upon a support.[10] "Human action depends upon all sorts of supports – it is always supported action."[11] A space emerges through the place then under negotiation and constitutes the material environment, the physical basis which supports action. The diversity of uses, experimentation, sociability, and conviviality require support via built structures. In the case of the University of Neighborhoods, a disused building had already been abandoned to disintegration and was designed, converted, and arranged to provide action with a support and hence to become a space. The photographic images of the University of Neighborhoods testified to the value of its use.

In June of 2013, I was invited to speak at the SEEDS Conference that took place in the University of Neighborhoods. At this small-scale international conference, which resembled a workshop, Regina Bittner spoke about "learning from… urban production". One of her arguments appeared central to me, and it forms my point of departure for the key scene on the importance of architectural photography in relation to the production of the discourse of the history of modernism in architectural history. There was, she argued, no one-sided modernism. Both from the perspective of historical materialism as well as from that of a history of Western ideas, modernism was always ambivalent. And this ambivalence is not invisible. It is exposed in the gaps, the omissions, the margins, at the sides.

But I don't want to jump ahead now and speak of this ambivalence and its esthetic and epistemological trouble; instead, we remain for the moment with the distortions of one-sidedness. Bittner explains that we must assume that modernity had two sides. And the terms she uses to refer to these two sides involve a spatial dimension, i.e., a front and a back. The front is turned toward a hegemonic history, or formulated conversely, the front is the side toward which a hegemonic history is turned and which is therefore presumed to be familiar. The rear is turned away from this hegemonic history; it is the side from which the traditional architectural history has turned away and therefore can be presumed to be unknown.

Bittner presents her argument with a striking example. With reference to the Dessau-Törten Estate III. 3 designed by Walter Gropius, she shows how a visual

Im Juni 2013 war ich eingeladen, auf der SEEDS-Konferenz zu sprechen, die in der Universität der Nachbarschaften stattfand. Auf dieser internationalen Konferenz, die in kleinem Rahmen stattfand und einem Workshop ähnelte, sprach Regina Bittner über das Thema „Learning from (…) urban production". Von ihrem Vortrag ist mir ein Argument zentral in Erinnerung geblieben, von dem ausgehend sich eine Schlüsselszene für die Bedeutung der Architekturfotografie in Hinblick auf die Herstellung des Diskurses der Architekturgeschichte der Moderne ausmachen lässt: Es habe keine einseitige Moderne gegeben. Sowohl aus der Perspektive des historischen Materialismus als auch aus der Perspektive einer westlichen Ideengeschichte betrachtet, sei die Moderne immer zwiespältig gewesen. Dieser Zwiespalt sei nicht unsichtbar. Er zeige sich in den Lücken, in den Auslassungen, in den Rändern, an den Seiten.

Doch ich möchte nicht weiter vorgreifen, noch nicht vom Zwiespalt und seiner ästhetischen und epistemologischen Bedrängnis sprechen, sondern bei der Verwerfung der Einseitigkeit bleiben. Bittner führte aus, man müsse davon ausgehen, dass es zwei Seiten der Moderne gegeben habe. Die Bezeichnungen, die sie für diese beiden Seiten verwendete, hatten eine räumliche Dimension: die Vorderseite und die Rückseite. Die Vorderseite ist die der hegemonialen Geschichte zugewandte, oder umgekehrt formuliert, die Vorderseite ist jene Seite, der sich die hegemoniale Geschichte zugewandt hat und die damit als bekannt vorausgesetzt werden kann. Die Rückseite ist die der hegemonialen Geschichte abgewandte, von der sich die traditionelle Architekturgeschichtsschreibung abgewandt hat und die damit als unbekannt vorausgesetzt werden kann.

Dieses Argument erläuterte Bittner eindrücklich durch ein konkretes Beispiel. Sie zeigte anhand der von Walter Gropius geplanten Siedlung Dessau-Törten **Abb.3** auf, wie die visuelle Überlieferungstradition ein bestimmtes Bild der Architektur der Moderne konstituierte und weitgehend prägte. Auf der offiziellen Website des Bauhauses Dessau findet sich folgende Kurzdarstellung: „Die von 1926 bis 1928 im Auftrag der Stadt Dessau gebaute Siedlung Törten entstand im Rahmen des Reichsheimstättengesetzes, d.h., die Häuser waren von Anfang an im Besitz der Bewohner. Mit der ‚halbländlichen' Siedlung wollte das Bauhaus Probleme des preisgünstigen Massenwohnungsbaus praktisch lösen. (…) In insgesamt drei Bauabschnitten entstanden 314 Reihenhäuser, die je

tradition of transmission constituted and to a large extent shaped a specific image of modernism. The official website of the Dessau Bauhaus features the following brief description: "Commissioned by the municipality of Dessau and built from 1926 to 1928, the Törten Estate was conceived within the framework of the Reichsheimstättengesetz (State Home Law), which meant that the houses were owned by the residents from the outset. With the 'suburban estate', the Bauhaus sought a practical solution to the problem of building affordable housing for the masses … In three phases of construction, 314 terraced houses were built with a floor space of between 57 and 75 m², according to the type of house. Different variants of the house types were built in an extensive trial set up in 1927 by the Reichsforschungsgesellschaft für Wirtschaftlichkeit im Bau- und Wohnungswesen (Imperial Research Society for Economic Efficiency in Building and Housing), to provide information on the rational manufacture of residential housing, and also on the suitability of new building materials and industrial products."[12] In the photographs, which have become a part of architectural history, it is the front that is visible; bright, ordered, cubic. This side of modernism is the one that has grown familiar, visible. "Gropius designed an estate of terraced houses with kitchen gardens measuring between 350 and 400 m² to grow vegetables and practice small-scale animal husbandry, thus supporting self-sufficiency."[13] Cultivated in the kitchen gardens set on the rear of the houses were potatoes, cauliflower, kale, beans, cabbage, and beets. In German, the expression "cabbage and beets" refers to things being "topsy-turvy." That is, planted together rather than separately, as crops normally are, they stand for confusion, chaos,

3

nach Haustyp zwischen 57 und 75 qm Wohnfläche aufweisen. Die Haustypen wurden in verschiedenen Varianten gebaut, um in einem ab 1927 angelegten umfangreichen Versuchsprogramm der Reichsforschungsgesellschaft für Wirtschaftlichkeit im Bau- und Wohnungswesen Aufschlüsse über eine rationelle Herstellung von Wohnbauten, aber auch über die Eignung neuer Baustoffe und Industrieprodukte zu erhalten."[12] Auf den Fotografien, die in die Architekturgeschichte eingegangen sind, ist die Vorderseite zu sehen; hell, geordnet, kubisch. Diese Seite der Moderne ist die bekannte, die sichtbar gewordene. „Gropius entwarf eine Reihenhaussiedlung mit Nutzgärten von jeweils 350 bis 400 qm für den Gemüseanbau und die Kleintierhaltung zur Selbstversorgung."[13] In den an der Rückseite gelegenen Nutzgärten wurden Kartoffeln, Blumenkohl, Grünkohl, Bohnen, Kraut und Rüben angepflanzt. Die sprichwörtlich gewordene Wendung von „Kraut und Rüben", die gemeinsam angebaut wurden (im Gegensatz zu anderen Feldfrüchten, die voneinander getrennt wurden), verweist auf Durcheinander, Chaos, Ungeordnetes. Diese Seite der Moderne ist die unbekannte, die unsichtbar gebliebene. Die drei Eigenschaften – hell, geordnet, kubisch –, die der Vorderseite als Kurzbeschreibung zugeordnet wurden, sind in der Architekturgeschichte sichtbar. Die Rückseite muss hier aus Mangel an Bildmaterial ohne Kurzbeschreibung bleiben und wird damit der Vorstellung der Leserinnen und Leser überlassen.

Ich möchte diese Vorderseite und diese Rückseite nochmals, und zwar aus einer historisch-materialistischen Perspektive, analysieren. Die Vorderseite ist auch die gebaute Manifestation der fordistischen Produktion, in der die der Rationalität der Architektur der Moderne mit der arbeitsteiligen und effizienzsteigernden Ökonomie ihrer kapitalistischen Produktionsweise korreliert. „Walter Gropius (…) wendete bei der Wohnsiedlung in Dessau-Törten das tayloristische System sowie Fords Methode der Fließbandproduktion auf beinahe wörtliche Weise an: Er verlegte die Fabrik zur Herstellung der Elemente auf das Baugelände und zog die in zwei parallelen Reihen angeordneten Reihenhäuser, in Etappen unterteilt, schrittweise hoch."[14] Die Rückseite der Nutzgärten hingegen ist die wachsende Manifestation einer auf Subsistenzwirtschaft[15] beruhenden Produktionsweise. Im Vergleich zur fordistischen Fabrikarbeit[16], die durch die Vorderseite symbolisiert wird, steht diese für die dem

disorder. This side of modernism is the one that has remained unfamiliar, invisible.

The three characteristics (bright, ordered, cubic), which I attributed above to the front, are visible in architectural history. Given the lack of documentary material, however, the rear remains deprived of a brief description and is hence left to the reader's imagination.

I would like to reanalyze this front and back, this time from a historical-materialist perspective. The front is also the built manifestation of Fordist production, where the rationality of modernist architecture corresponds to the economics of capitalist production, with its emphasis on the division of labor and the enhancement of efficiency. "For the Dessau-Törten Estate Walter Gropius… used the Taylorist system, along with Ford's method of assembly line production, in an almost literal way: In order to manufacture the elements, he shifted the factory to the building site, raising two parallel rows of houses by stages, step by step."[14] The rear sides, with their kitchen gardens, on the other hand, were a growing manifestation of a mode of production based on a subsistence economy.[15] In comparison to Fordist factory work[16], symbolized by the front, the rear stands for the reproductive realm to which gardening work is assigned. If the front is turned toward modernism and embodies an economically rational architectural production in esthetic terms, then the rear is, in terms of reception history, turned away from it. These binary dichotomies can be summed up as follows: visible – invisible; known – unknown; ordered – disordered; factory work – gardening work; productive work – reproductive work; remunerated labor – unremunerated labor; Fordist capitalism – pre-Fordist subsistence economics; urban – rural. While this can be demonstrated with reference to the individual case of the Dessau-Törten Estate, it also sheds light on the formation of a discourse that has been decisive for the architecture of modernism as a whole, namely, the difference between a hegemonic, visible front and a marginalized, invisible rear. Architectural photography, at least what was published in the context of a hegemonic architectural history, is located on the front, that of visibility. It participated in generating a hegemonic discourse that was established not least of all through acts of visibility. That which was in step with the times, which corresponded to contemporary

reproduktiven Bereich zugeordneten Gartenarbeit. Wurde die Vorderseite die der Moderne zugewandte, die den Rationalismus einer ökonomisierten Architekturproduktion ästhetisch verkörperte, so wurde die Rückseite rezeptionsgeschichtlich die der Moderne abgewandte. Die binären Dichotomien lassen sich wie folgt zuspitzen: sichtbar – unsichtbar; bekannt – unbekannt; geordnet – ungeordnet; Fabrikarbeit – Gartenarbeit; produktive Arbeit – reproduktive Arbeit; bezahlte Arbeit – unbezahlte Arbeit; fordistischer Kapitalismus – präfordistische Subsistenzwirtschaft; urban – ländlich. Wiewohl dies am einzelnen Beispiel der Siedlung Dessau-Törten gezeigt wird, lässt sich hier durchaus die Formation eines Diskurses ableiten, der für die Architektur der Moderne als bestimmend gilt: die Differenz zwischen hegemonialer, sichtbarer Vorderseite und marginalisierter, unsichtbarer Rückseite. Die Architekturfotografie, zumindest die im Kontext hegemonialer Architekturgeschichten veröffentlichten Fotografien, stand dabei auf der Seite der Vorderseite, auf der Seite der Sichtbarkeit. Sie war an der Erzeugung eines hegemonialen Diskurses beteiligt, der nicht zuletzt über das Sichtbarwerden etabliert wurde. Das, was der Höhe der Zeit, der vorherrschenden Produktionsweise und ihrer Ökonomie entsprach, die Vorderseite, wurde aufgenommen, abgelichtet, vervielfältigt. Dies ging auf Kosten der Nutzerinnen und Nutzer. Dort, wo der Ort, den die Architektur hervorbrachte, durch Handlung zum Raum gemacht wurde, um mit de Certeau zu argumentieren, konnte kein visueller Mehrwert auf der Höhe der Zeit abgeschöpft werden. Deshalb musste die Architektur selbst zum visuellen Hauptakteur werden, der als Ort im Bild fixiert bleibt und nicht durch Nutzung transformierbarer Raum wird. Die Architektur, die mit Butler gedacht, auch politisch werden könnte, indem sie als physisch-materielle Unterstützung menschlichen Handelns zur Erscheinung gebracht wird, bleibt in den Konventionen des Diskurses apolitisch und zeigt sich nicht in der Dimension, in der Menschen von ihr als Abhängige unterstützt werden können. Nicht zuletzt sind die hellen Kuben der Siedlung Dessau-Törten zur Ikone der Moderne avanciert, weil ihre Vorderseite durch die Fotografien zu zirkulieren begann. Hier wird deutlich, wie die Architekturfotografie eine zentrale Rolle für die Formierung des Diskurses der Architektur der Moderne als Bildmacht spielte. Am Beispiel der Siedlung Dessau-Törten lässt sich daher die diskursive Formierung der Überlieferung von

developments, to the predominant production methods and their economics, to the front, was photographed, illuminated, reproduced. This was done at the expense of users. The place that generated the architecture was converted through negotiation into a space, to argue with de Certeau, one that was nevertheless unable to generate any visual added value in conformity with the standards of the times. Therefore, the architecture itself had become the main visual protagonist and remained fixed in the image as a place, never becoming a space that was transformable through use. According to the conventions of the discourse, the architecture – which, in Butler's thinking, could also become political, i.e., by attaining visibility as the physical-material support of human action – remained apolitical, never revealing the dimension in which people drew support from it or became dependent upon it. The pale cubic forms of the Dessau-Törten Estate advanced to the status of icons of modernism not least of all because their fronts began to circulate via the photographic medium. Now it becomes clear how architectural photography, with its iconic power, played a central role in shaping the discourse of architectural modernism. The discursive formation that controls the transmission of built architecture becomes visible through this reference to the Dessau-Törten Estate. This leads to more general inferences concerning the conventions in the Western historiography of architecture. The key to this key scene lies in architectural photography. That is, the front attains representation while the rear is never photographed. The front becomes hegemonic; the rear remains marginal.

And now I turn to the building in Belgrade mentioned at the beginning. It is known to me through a lecture and through personal conversations with the artist Dušica Dražić, who showed me photographs of her installation work *Blueprint*. The international symposium *Memory of the City – Participative Policies and Practices in Service of Activation of Memory in the Development of the City* was held on September 12 and 13, 2011, in the Cultural Center in Belgrade. Dražić was to have spoken about her work as part of this symposium but was prevented from delivering her lecture by ill health. Zoran Erić, the curator of the Center for Visual Culture of the Museum of Contemporary Art in Belgrade, spoke in her stead about *Blueprint*, whose 14 photographs

gebauter Architektur nachvollziehen. Dies lässt allgemeine Rückschlüsse auf die Konventionen der westlichen Architekturgeschichtsschreibung zu. Der Schlüssel zu dieser Schlüsselszene liegt in der Architekturfotografie: Die Vorderseite gelangte zur Darstellung. Die Rückseite wurde nicht aufgenommen. Die Vorderseite wurde hegemonial. Die Rückseite blieb marginal.

Ich möchte mich nun dem eingangs angekündigten Gebäude in Belgrad zuwenden. Es ist mir aus einem Vortrag sowie aus persönlichen Gesprächen mit der Künstlerin Dušiza Dražić bekannt, in denen sie mir Fotografien ihrer installativen Arbeit *Blueprint* zeigte. Am 12. und 13. September 2011 fand im Kulturzentrum in Belgrad das internationale Symposium *Memory of the City – Participative Policies and Practices in Service of Activation of Memory in the Development of the City* statt. Im Rahmen dieses Symposiums hätte Dušiza Dražić über ihre Arbeit sprechen sollen; aus Krankheitsgründen konnte sie den geplanten Vortrag jedoch nicht halten. Zoran Erić, Kurator am Zentrum für Visuelle Kultur des Museums für Zeitgenössische Kunst Belgrad, sprach an ihrer Stelle über Dražićs Arbeit *Blueprint*, die in einer Serie von 14 Fotografien ein typisches altes Belgrader Haus im Prozess seines Verschwindens dokumentiert. Auf der ersten Fotografie sehen wir ein baufälliges vernakulares Belgrader Haus. **Abb. 4.** Die folgenden beiden Aufnahmen zeigen den verlassenen Zustand, den Zustand nach der Nutzung. Die nächsten vier Aufnahmen dokumentieren den Abriss, die Zerstörung. **Abb. 5.** Die folgenden zwei Aufnahmen zeigen den Abtransport des Abrissmaterials auf einem Lastwagen. Die nächste Aufnahme zeigt das Abladen des Bauschutts in der Galerie. Darauf folgt ein gezeichneter Grundriss der ehemaligen Räume, die nun in Schutt aufgegangen sind. Die letzten vier Fotografien zeigen den Boden des Galerieraums, der mit den Abrissmaterialien gefüllt ist. Über diese bewegen sich die Besucherinnen und Besucher der Installation. Dieses Haus steht stellvertretend für viele alte Häuser, die zu Beginn des 21. Jahrhunderts in Belgrad vom Abriss bedroht sind. Der Systemwechsel zeigt sich großmaßstäblich im Umbau der Stadt Belgrad. Zoran Erić und Stefan Vuković sprechen davon, dass an die Stelle von dionyischem Sozialismus räuberischer Kapitalismus getreten sei.[17] „With the installation *Blueprint* Dražić not only addresses the socio-economical context of the transformation and disappearance of old Belgrade districts

document the disappearance of an ordinary old house in Belgrade. In the first photograph, we see a dilapidated, vernacular Belgrade house. III. 4. The succeeding pair of images shows its neglected condition, that is its condition after use. The following four photographs document its demolition, its destruction. III. 5. The next two show the removal of the resultant debris on a truck. The next photograph shows the unloading of this construction waste in the gallery. This is followed by a drawn floor plan of the former rooms, now transformed into debris. The four concluding photographs show the floor of the gallery space, now filled with this demolition material. Visitors to the installation are making their way across it. This house represents many old houses in Belgrade that are threatened by demolition in the early 21st century. The transition to a new system is visible on a large scale in Belgrade's transformation. Zoran Erić and Stefan Vuković speak of the way in which Dionysian socialism is being supplanted by predatory capitalism.[17] "With the installation *Blueprint*, Dražić not only addresses the socio-economic context of the transformation and disappearance of old Belgrade districts, but also points to the ways in which these changes influence the relationship between a resident and the city. By reconstructing the moment of disappearance and demolition of a typical family house, Dražić tries to capture a moment of change."[18] The house is disassembled into its constituent elements; these are then transported to an art space. It becomes material once again. The place where the house became a space through action, and which offered a family support for its activities, has been demolished. It is a house after use. In the gallery, it becomes accessible. People bend down, picking up pieces of material.

4

but also points to the ways in which these changes influence the relationship between a resident and the city. By reconstructing the moment of disappearance and demolition of a typical family house, Dražić tries to capture a moment of change."[18] Das Haus ist in seine Bestandteile zerlegt; diese werden in den Kunstraum abtransportiert. Es ist wieder Material. Der Ort, an dem es durch Handeln zu Raum wurde und einer Familie die Unterstützung für dieses Handeln bot, ist abgerissen. Es ist ein Haus nach der Nutzung. In der Galerie wird es begehbar. Die Menschen bücken sich, greifen die Materialien an. Diese werden zum Erinnerungswert, die physisch-materielle Unterstützung der Erinnerung. Paradoxerweise heißt die Arbeit *Blueprint*: Entwurf, Plan, Blaupause.

Abschließend möchte ich die drei verschiedenen Funktionen, die die Fotografie von Architektur in den von mir ausgewählten Beispielen übernimmt, im Vergleich miteinander darstellen. Die Fotografien der Universität der Nachbarschaften mussten das Gebäude nicht in den Vordergrund rücken; es war bereits jenseits der Gebäudeverwertungsinteressen angelangt. Der Zustand der Restnutzung vor dem Abriss ermöglichte der Nutzung, in den Vordergrund zu treten. Die Aufnahmen der Siedlung Dessau-Törten zeigen, wie bedeutsam die Fotografie für die Formation des Diskurses der Architektur der Moderne war und diese auf der Höhe der fordistischen Produktionsweise ihrer Zeit zeigte, indem sie die Vorderseite bildmächtig werden ließ und die Rückseite verschwinden ließ. Das vernakulare Belgrader Haus gewinnt durch die Fotografien ein Nachleben nach der Nutzung. Kapitalinteressen und Bodenspekulation, so lässt sich vermuten, brachten es zum Verschwinden. Es war nicht mehr zeitgemäß. Die Fotografien dokumentieren das Verschwinden der Nutzung als Erinnerung, indem sie an deren (Un-)Möglichkeit gemahnen. Um ein Verständnis für die jeweils vorherrschenden historischen Verhältnisse zwischen Architektur, Nutzung, Ökonomie, Politik, Raum, Ort und Handlung zu erlangen, enthalten Architekturfotografien die entscheidenden Hinweise auf die hegemonialen Diskurse, an deren Formation, Offenlegung, Kritik und Tradierung sie Anteil haben.

These then acquire a memorial value, become the physical-material supports of memory. Paradoxically, the work bears the title *Blueprint*, i.e., design, floor plan.

In closing, I want to compare the three different functions photography assumes for architecture in the examples I have selected above. The photographs of the University of Neighborhoods had to avoid allowing the building to emerge in the foreground; it was already positioned beyond the interests of economic valorization. The condition of its residual use prior to demolition made it possible for use to emerge in the foreground. The photographs of the Dessau-Törten Estate illustrate the significance of photography in the formation of the discourse of architectural modernism and display it in a way that emblematizes the Fordist mode of production, i.e., by endowing the front with a powerful visual impact while making the rear to disappear. Via photography, the vernacular Belgrade house acquires an afterlife that occurs post-use. The interests of capitalism and real estate speculation, it can be assumed, brought about its disappearance. It is no longer up-to-date. The photographs document its disappearing usefulness in the form of memory, reminding us of its (im)possibility. In order to arrive at an understanding of the historical relations that prevailed respectively between architecture, use, economics, politics, space, place, and action, it is architectural photography that provides us with the decisive references to the hegemonial discourse that contributes to its formation, its exposure, its critique, and its transmission.

5

1 Freie und Hansestadt Hamburg, Behörde für Stadtentwicklung und Umwelt
(Hg.), *Sprung über die Elbe. Hamburg auf dem Weg zur Internationalen Bauaus-
stellung – IBA Hamburg 2013*, Freie und Hansestadt Hamburg, Behörde für
Stadtentwicklung und Umwelt, Hamburg, 2005.

2 IBA Hamburg GmbH (Hg.), *Experiment auf der Insel. Temporäre Intervention
auf dem Grundstück Rotenhäuser Damm in Wilhelmsburg*. Wettbewerbs-
dokumentation. Kooperationsprojekt der IBA Hamburg GmbH und der Hafencity
Universität Hamburg, Hamburg 2008, S. 3.

3 Vgl. a.a.O., S.16.

4 Anton Reinig et al, *Grenzposten. Betrieb und Nutzung, Wettbewerbsbeitrag
Experiment auf der Insel*, 2007.

5 Die geplanten Bauvorhaben wurden in einer öffentlichen Ausstellung als
Werkschau IBA von 6. Juni bis 23. September 2010 in Kunstverein Hamburg an
Hand von Plänen, Renderings und Modellen präsentiert.

6 http://udn.hcu-hamburg.de/en/?cat=3 (aufgesucht am 4. Mai 2015).

7 Dies zeigt sich auf den dokumentarischen Fotografien, die das Projekt
beispielsweise auf der Website der IBA vorstellen.

8 Michel de Certeau, *Die Kunst des Handelns*, Merve Verlag, Berlin, 1988, S. 218.
Das französische Original erschien im Jahr 1980. Dieses Buch war leitende
theoretische Grundlage für die Arbeitsweisen und Handlungspraxen, die von der
Universität der Nachbarschaften erprobt wurden.

9 Judith Butler, „Bodies in Alliance and the Politics of the Street", in:
Meg McLagan und Yates McKee (Hg.), *Sensible Politics. The Visual Culture of
Nongovernmental Activism*, Zone Books, New York, 2012, S.117.

10 Ebd., S.118.

11 a.a.O.

12 http://www.bauhaus-dessau.de/siedlung-dessau-toerten.html
(aufgesucht am 4. Mai 2015).

13 Ebd.

14 Christoph Wieser, „Wegbereiter und Projektionsfläche: Vereinnahmung des
Ingenieurs im Neuen Bauen", in: Aita Flury (Hg.), *Kooperation. Zur Zusammenarbeit von Ingenieur und Architekt*, Birkhäuser Verlag, Basel, 2011, S. 38.

15 Für eine Darstellung der Subsistenzperspektive siehe: Veronika Bennholdt-
Thomsen und Maria Mies, *Eine Kuh für Hillary – Die Subsistenzperspektive*,
Frauenoffensive, München, 1997.

16 Für eine Darstellung des Fordismus siehe: Institut für kritische Theorie,
Thomas Barfuss (Hg.), Antonio Gramsci, *Amerikanismus und Fordismus*,
Argument Verlag, Hamburg, 2007.

17 Zoran Erić, Stefan Vuković, *From Dionysian Socialism to Predatory Capitalism*,
Belgrade Museum of Contemporary Art, Belgrad, 2012.

18 Slavica Radišić, Blueprint, https://dusicadrazic.wordpress.com/portfolio/
blueprint/ (aufgesucht am 4. Mai 2015).

Fotonachweise

Abb. 1 *Wilhelmsburg Orchestra*, eine Veranstaltung der Universität der
Nachbarschaften im Rahmen der Aktion 48 Stunden Wilhelmsburg, 2011,
Foto: HCU/UdN (HafenCity Universität/Universität der Nachbarschaften)

Abb. 2 Universität der Nachbarschaften, *Strickbaumhaus*, Sommerbaucamp
2012, Foto: Benjamin Becker

Abb. 3 Walter Gropius, Siedlung Dessau Törten, Häuser des Typs 1928 –
Eingangsseite, 1928, Fotograf unbekannt, Bauhaus-Archiv Berlin

Abb. 4 Dušica Dražić, *Blueprint*, 2011

Abb. 5 Dušica Dražić, *Blueprint*, 2011

1 Freie und Hansestadt Hamburg, Behörde für Stadtentwicklung und Umwelt
(ed.), *Sprung über die Elbe. Hamburg auf dem Weg zur Internationalen Bauausstellung – IBA Hamburg 2013*, Hamburg, Freie und Hansestadt Hamburg,
Behörde für Stadtentwicklung und Umwelt, Hamburg, 2005.

2 IBA Hamburg GmbH (ed.), *Experiment auf der Insel. Temporäre Intervention auf
dem Grundstück Rotenhäuser Damm in Wilhelmsburg*, competition documentation,
a cooperation project of the IBA Hamburg GmbH and the HafenCity University
Hamburg, Hamburg, 2008, p.3.

3 Cf. ibid., p.16.

4 Anton Reinig et al, *Grenzposten. Betrieb und Nutzung, Wettbewerbsbeitrag
Experiment auf der Insel*, 2007.

5 The planned building project was presented in a public exhibition of the IBA
that ran from June 6 to September 23, 2010 at the Kunstverein Hamburg and
included plans, renderings, and models.

6 http://udn.hcu-hamburg.de/en/?cat=3 (visited on May 4, 2015)

7 This is shown in the documentary photographs presented, for example, on
the IBA website.

8 Michel de Certeau, *The Practice of Everyday Life*, University of California Press,
1984, p.117. The French original appeared in 1980; the German version (*Die Kunst
des Handelns*, Merve Verlag, Berlin, 1988) constituted a guiding theoretical basis
for the working approach and practices tested by the University of Neighborhoods.

9 Judith Butler, "Bodies in Alliance and the Politics of the Street" in:
Meg McLagan and Yates McKee (eds.), *Sensible Politics. The Visual Culture of
Nongovernmental Activism*, Zone Books, New York, 2012, p.117.

10 Ibid. p.118.

11 Ibid.

12 http://www.bauhaus-dessau.de/siedlung-dessau-toerten.html
(visited on June 18, 2015).

13 Ibid.

14 Christoph Wieser, "Wegbereiter und Projektionsfläche: Vereinnahmung
des Ingenieurs im Neuen Bauen" in: Aita Flury (ed.) *Cooperation. The Engineer
and the Architect*, Birkhäuser Verlag, Basel, 2011, p.38.

15 For a discussion of this subsistence perspective, see Veronika Bennholdt-
Thomsen and Maria Mies, *Eine Kuh für Hillary – Die Subsistenzperspektive*,
Frauenoffensive, Munich, 1997.

16 For a discussion of Fordism, see Institut für kritische Theorie, Thomas Barfuss
(ed.), *Antonio Gramsci: Amerikanismus und Fordismus*, Argument Verlag,
Hamburg, 2007.

17 Zoran Erić, Stefan Vuković: *From Dionysian Socialism to Predatory
Capitalism*, Belgrade Museum of Contemporary Art, Belgrade, 2012.

18 Slavica Radišić: Blueprint, https://dusicadrazic.wordpress.com/portfolio/
blueprint/ (visited on May 4, 2015).

Picture Credits

Ill. 1 *Wilhelmsburg Orchestra*, an event at the University of Neighborhoods as
part of the 48 Stunden Wilhelmsburg action, 2011, photo: HCU/UdN (HafenCity
Universität/University of Neighborhoods)

Ill. 2 University of Neighborhoods, *Strickbaumhaus*, summer building camp, 2012,
photo: Benjamin Becker

Ill. 3 Walter Gropius, Dessau Törten Estate, houses of the 1928 type: entrance
side, 1928, photographer unknown, Bauhaus-Archiv Berlin

Ill. 4 Dušica Dražić, *Blueprint*, 2011

Ill. 5 Dušica Dražić, *Blueprint*, 2011

Frequenz
Frequency

: Nutzungsspuren
: Traces of Use

Geht es um Wertsteigerung, so kann das Foto eines Gebäudes nicht oft genug in den Medien gezeigt werden. Während die starke Nutzung eines Fotos also den Wert eines Bauwerks hebt, sinkt er – zumindest in den Augen vieler Architektinnen und Architekten – durch die extensive oder unangemessene Nutzung des Gebäudes selbst. Begriffe wie „Übernutzung" oder „Verschandelung" zeugen davon. Viele Gebäude werden sicherheitshalber im Ursprungszustand dokumentiert, unbeeinträchtigt von Gebrauchs- und Verschleißerscheinungen. Der äußerst flüchtige Moment zwischen Fertigstellung und Besiedelung, wenn die Architektur noch Versprechen ist, gebaute Potenzialität, wird eingefangen. Ein kostbarer Moment in einer Zeit, in der bereits auf den digitalen Vorabvisualisierungen Kinder, Haustiere und Pflanzen zu sehen sind, in der das echte Leben simuliert und vorausberechnet wird. Manchmal sind die Fotografinnen und Fotografen sogar zu früh zur Stelle, noch bevor alle Oberflächen versiegelt und alle Werkzeuge verräumt sind.

Anders verhält es sich mit historischen Bauwerken: Wird durch eine hohe Frequenz in der Architekturgeschichte erst einmal ein Kultstatus erreicht, dann erhöhen Spuren von Abnutzung die Aura der fotografierten Architektur. Erst der abgetretene, fleckige Boden, erst die unregelmäßig verdrehten Stühle, zurückgeblieben von davoneilenden Abgeordneten, machen den Parlamentssaal zu einem historischen Ort. Erst die geballte Versammlung der Ventilatoren befragt den Siegeszug der Moderne im globalen Süden. Manchmal verraten nur ein paar Blumentöpfe, dass Menschen beginnen, sich in einer Megastruktur aus Beton einzurichten. Manchmal kehren die Fotografinnen und Fotografen zurück und fangen die Vielfalt der privaten Balkonreservate für uns ein. In Wien scheint ein transparenter Kubus noch auf den Sturm des urbanen Lebens zu warten, während in Hongkong die Glasfassade eines Apple Stores unter dem Ansturm der Massen fast zu bersten droht. AF

When it comes to enhancing value, a photograph of a building cannot be shown often enough in the media. While the intensive use of a specific photograph elevates a building's value, that same value declines – at least in the eyes of many architects – as a consequence of the extensive or inappropriate use of the architecture itself. Terms such as "overuse" and "disfigurement" testify to this. As a precaution, many buildings are documented in their original states, unaffected by traces of use or signs of wear. Captured here is the extraordinarily fleeting moment between completion and occupation, when the architecture is still a promise, built potentiality. It is a precious moment in time when children, pets, and plants are already displayed via digital previsualization, when genuine life is simulated and anticipated. At times, the photographer even turns up too early, before all of the surfaces have been sealed and the construction equipment cleared away.

Things are different with historic buildings. If cult status is attained in architectural history only through high-frequency exposure, then it is precisely the traces of wear and tear that heighten the aura of photographed architecture. It is only the well-trodden, stained floor, the erratically positioned chairs, the presence of lingering delegates and those hurrying away that make the assembly hall of a parliament building a historic location. Only the clenched collection of fans questions the victory of modernism in the globalized South. At times, only a couple of flower pots betray human attempts to adapt a concrete megastructure. At times, the photographer returns to capture for us the great variety on view in a preserve of private balconies. In Vienna, a transparent cube seems to await the tumult of urban life, while in Hongkong the glass facade of an Apple Store almost threatens to shatter under the onslaught of masses of shoppers. AF

Foto Photo Manfred Seidl, 2008
Architektur Architecture gerner°gerner plus
Projekt Project THU – Wohnbau Housing Estate
Thürnlhof-West, Wien (AT), 2007

Foto Photo Stefan Oláh, aus from Einfache Bauten –
Simple Structures MAKZINE#1, 2012
Architektur Architecture Peter von Nobile
Projekt Project Theseustempel Temple of Theseus,
Wien (AT), 1823

36

Foto Photo Dietmar Tollerian/Archipicture, 2012
Architektur Architecture Kaufmann & Partner Architekten
Projekt Project City Center One Zagreb East,
Zagreb (HR), 2012

Frequenz: Nutzungsspuren

Foto Photo Pez Hejduk, 2003
Architektur Architecture Adolf Krischanitz,
Ulrich Huhs
Landschaftsarchitektur Landscape Architecture
Anna Detzlhofer
Projekt Project Wohnhausanlage Housing estate
Tokiostraße, Wien (AT), 2003

Foto Photo Markus Kaiser, 2011
Architektur Architecture AllesWirdGut
Projekt Project Open Air Festspielarena im Römer-
steinbruch Open air festival arena at the Roman Quarry,
St. Margarethen (AT), 2008

Foto Photo Stefan Oláh, aus from Österreichische
Architektur der Fünfziger Jahre (Austrian architecture
of the 1950s), 2011
Architektur Architecture Max Fellerer, Eugen Wörle
Projekt Project Parlament Parliament building,
Sitzungssaal des Nationalrates Assembly hall,
National Assembly, Wien (AT), 1955–1961

Foto **Photo** Peter Eder, 1996
Architektur **Architecture** Le Corbusier
Projekt **Project** Mill Owners' Association Building,
Ahmedabad (IN), 1954

Foto **Photo** Pez Hejduk, 2005
Architektur **Architecture** Erich Boltenstern
Projekt **Project** Büro und Wohnhaus **Office and**
apartment house Erich Boltenstern, Wien (AT), 1964

Foto Photo Gisela Erlacher, 2012
Architektur Architecture Pelli Clarke Pelli
Architects
Projekt Project International Finance Centre IFC,
Hong Kong (RC), 2004

Foto Photo Markus Bstieler, aus from Dokumentation
Documentation Clemens Holzmeister, Halle Hall
Baur-Foradori, Innsbruck (AT), 2013

Foto **Photo** Margherita Spiluttini, 1997

Architektur **Architecture** Franz Anton Danne, Fresco von

Fresco by Anton Herzog

Projekt **Project** Ehemaliger Lesesaal der Alten Universität

Wien **Old University, former reading room**, Zwischennutzung

als Tischtennishalle des Polizeisportvereins **Temporary use**

by Police Sports Club, Wien (AT), 1624

Foto Photo Margherita Spiluttini, Courtesy
Christine König Galerie, 2005
Architektur Architecture Herzog & de Meuron
Projekt Project Tate Modern, London (GB), 2000

Foto Photo Pia Odorizzi, 2010
Architektur Architecture Delugan Meissl Associated
Architects
Projekt Project Brauerei Liesing – Wohn- und
Geschäftsgebäude Housing and office building,
Wien (AT), 2009

Frequenz: Nutzungsspuren

Foto Photo Stefan Oláh, aus from Einfache Bauten –
Simple Structures MAKZINE#1, 2012
Architektur Architecture Karl Schwanzer
Projekt Project Akademie für angewandte Kunst,
Zubau, Wien (AT), 1965

Foto Photo Peter Eder, 1996
Architektur Architecture Le Corbusier
Projekt Project Ahmedabad Museum,
Ahmedabad (IN), 1957

Foto Photo Markus Bstieler, aus from C.O.R.A.G. #01,
Gazzolo di Arcole (IT), 2003/2004

Foto Photo Gisela Erlacher, Naschmarkt,
Wien (AT), 1998

Foto Photo Rupert Steiner, 2001

Architektur Architecture Valie Export, Silja Tillner

Projekt Project Kubus Export – Der Transparente Raum

(The transparent room), Wien (AT), 1999

54

Foto Photo Günter Richard Wett, aus from
Spurensuche in Brasilien (Searching for traces in Brazil) –
Artigas, Bo Bardi, Mendes da Rocha, 2008
Architektur Architecture Vilanova Artigas
Projekt Project Estação Rodoviária de Jaú
Bus terminal, Jaú (BR), 1973

55

Foto Photo Markus Kaiser, 2014

Architektur Architecture Architektur Consult

Projekt Project Styria Media Center, Graz (AT), 2014

Foto Photo Margherita Spiluttini, 2002
Architektur Architecture ARTEC Architekten,
Bettina Götz + Richard Manahl
Projekt Project Wohnbebauung Residential area
Laxenburgerstraße, Wien (AT), 2001

Frequenz

Frequency

: meistgenutzt | ungenutzt
: Most-used | Unused

Manche Architekturfotos sind wie Musikhits. Ähnlich wie einzelne Songs eines Albums im Powerplay von Radio und YouTube in den Charts nach oben gespült werden, macht häufig ein einzelnes Foto einer Serie Karriere. Ein Erfolgsfoto kann entscheidend zum Bekanntheitsgrad eines Gebäudes beitragen und sich verselbstständigen, denn die mediale Aufmerksamkeit sucht nach Eindeutigkeit und Wiedererkennbarkeit. Was ist nach den Kriterien der Redaktionen ein Erfolgsfoto? Welche Sehgewohnheiten bestimmen den Bilderkanon? Muss ein gutes Bild eine umfassende Beschreibung liefern oder darf es ein Geheimnis bewahren? Welcher Kontext ist genehm, welcher sollte besser ausgeblendet werden? Was unterscheidet eigentlich in den folgenden Bildpaaren die meistpublizierten Fotos von den Raritäten?

Die Ansicht eines nebelverhangenen Gebäudes kann mehr über dessen Charakter aussagen als ein scharfes Panoramabild. Dennoch findet sie nur selten ihren Weg in die Architekturmagazine. „Die subjektive Interpretation der Fotografin, die den surrealen Charakter des ufoartigen Porsche-Museums unterstreicht, unterliegt der scheinbar sachlichen und objektiven Fotografie, in der die Darstellungskonventionen gewahrt wurden", stellt Hubertus Adam, Direktor des Schweizerischen Architekturmuseums, mit Bedauern fest. Geht es also um die schnelle und eindeutige Lesbarkeit eines Gebäudes? Für die Architekturkritikerin Isabella Marboe vermittelt ein gutes Foto „ein Gefühl für die Architektur und bringt vieles auf den Punkt." Und sie zieht eine Analogie: Selbst komplexe architektonische Konzepte lassen sich vor Ort sofort begreifen. „Das gilt auch für ein gutes Foto." Oder gelten gar auch in der Architekturfotografie die Erfolgsrezepte Kinder und Tiere? Aber was, wenn das Haus „viel lebendiger ist als das Huhn", so der Architekturforscher Christian Kühn? Es bleibt die Frage, welche reizvollen Perspektiven in der Medialisierung verloren gehen. AF

Some architectural photos are like musical hits. Just as in the power play of radio and YouTube, an individual song can send an album rocketing up in the charts, an individual photo often establishes the career of an entire series. A successful photograph can contribute decisively to a building's degree of familiarity, and – given that media attention strives toward uniqueness and recognizability – even take on a life of its own. What, according to the criteria of the editorial offices, is a successful photo? Which viewing habits determine the canon of images? Need a good image provide us with an exhaustive depiction or can it safeguard its secrets? Which context is acceptable, which by preference suppressed? In the following pairs of images, what actually distinguishes the most-published photos from the rarities?

A view of a building veiled in fog can reveal more about its character than a sharply-focused panoramic image. Still the former rarely finds its way into architectural magazines. "A photographer's subjective interpretation, one that underscores the surreal character of the UFO-like Porsche Museum, loses out to the seemingly realistic, objective photograph, which respects the conventions of representation," Hubertus Adam, the Director of the Swiss Architecture Museum, notes with regret. Is it then a question of a building's rapid and unambiguous readability? For the architecture critic Isabella Marboe, a good photograph conveys "a feel for the architecture while encapsulating a great deal." And she draws an analogy: Even complex architectural concepts can be grasped on location immediately, and "the same is true for a good photograph." Or is the recipe for success, "children and animals," valid as well for architectural photography? And should the building prove "much livelier than the chicken," the architecture researcher Christian Kühn asks? It remains an open question which appealing perspectives are lost through mediatization. AF

In der folgenden Bildstrecke bekommt das von Architekturmedien vernachlässigte – das ungenutzte – Foto seinen Auftritt. Es steht jeweils an erster Stelle, während das meistgenutzte Foto derselben Serie auf Platz zwei folgt.

Featured in the following image sequence are photographs that have been neglected – were not used – by the architectural media. Each comes first in the respective group, and is then followed by the most-used photo from the same series, which is positioned second.

„1988 fotografierte Hans Danuser Peter Zumthors Kapelle Sogn Benedetg im Nebel, und diese atmosphärische Aufnahme wurde zur meistveröffentlichten seiner Zumthor-Serie, obwohl er gegen die ungeschriebenen Konventionen der Architekturfotografie verstoßen hatte: kein Nebel, kein Regen, kein Schnee. Dauerhaft verändert wurde die Optik der Architekturzeitschriften offensichtlich nicht: Bis heute wird die vorgeblich korrekte Totale, in der alle Details zu sehen sind, einem Bild vorgezogen, bei dem der Nebel sich des Gebäudes bemächtigt. Die subjektive Interpretation der Fotografin, die den surrealen Charakter des ufoartigen Porsche-Museums unterstreicht, unterliegt der scheinbar sachlichen und objektiven Fotografie, in der die Darstellungskonventionen gewahrt wurden. Bedauerlich, dass Architekturzeitschriften Fotos immer noch als Abbildungen der Wirklichkeit missverstehen, anstatt sie als deren Interpretation zu erkennen."

Hubertus Adam, Direktor des Schweizerischen Architekturmuseums Basel

“In 1988, Hans Danuser photographed Peter Zumthor's Kapelle Sogn Benedetg (Chapel of Saint Benedict) in the fog, and this atmospheric image became the most-published photograph from his Zumthor series, although it transgresses unwritten conventions of architectural photography, namely, no fog, no rain, no snow. Evidently the visual appearances of architectural periodicals were not really changed by it. To this day the purportedly total image, in which all details are visible, is preferred to one in which fog has enveloped a building. A photographer's subjective interpretation, one that underscores the surreal character of the UFO-like Porsche Museum, loses out to the seemingly realistic, objective photograph, which respects the conventions of representation. It is regrettable that architectural magazines always misunderstand photos as representations of reality instead of recognizing them as interpretations.”

Hubertus Adam, Director of the Swiss Architecture Museum in Basel

Foto Photo Hertha Hurnaus, 2008
Architektur Architecture Delugan Meissl Associated Architects
Projekt Project Porsche Museum, Stuttgart (DE), 2008

61

Foto Photo Margherita Spiluttini, 1998
Architektur Architecture Herzog & de Meuron
Projekt Project Haus House in Leymen,
Leymen (FR), 1997

„Ein Huhn. Immerhin. Da huscht es durchs Bild. Scheucht das alte Klischee auf, dass Architekturfotografie immer vergisst, das Leben zu zeigen. Tatsächlich? Ist das Haus, wie seine Rückseite zeigt, nicht viel lebendiger als das Huhn?"

Christian Kühn, Architekturkritiker und Architekturforscher

"A chicken. OK. It scampers around the image. Does it revive the old cliché according to which architectural photography always forgets to include life? Really? Isn't the house that exposes its rear more lively than the chicken?"

Christian Kühn, architectural critic and researcher

Foto Photo Margherita Spiluttini, 1998
Architektur Architecture ARTEC Architekten,
Bettina Götz + Richard Manahl
Projekt Project Haus House Zita Kern,
Raasdorf (AT), 1998

„Ungenutzt: Das Hauptaugenmerk dieses Fotos liegt auf der schroffen Berglandschaft, dem exponierten Standort der Seilbahnstation. Die Konstruktionselemente mit ihrer Bespannung aus durchsichtigen Membranen werden deutlich gezeigt. Da das Gebäude jedoch nur teilweise zu sehen ist, eignet sich dieses Foto eher als Ergänzung zu anderen, denn wenn man das Gebäude nicht kennt, könnte man sich speziell aufgrund des Maßstabsprungs zwischen der Felslandschaft im Vordergrund und der Seilbahnstation im Hintergrund fragen, welche Funktion das hinter den Steinblöcken verborgene Gebilde eigentlich erfüllt.

Meistgenutzt: Dass dieses Foto von der Bergstation der Gaislachkogl-Bahn das meistgenutzte ist, überrascht mich insofern nicht, als auch wir es mehrfach als ‚Imagefoto' ausgewählt haben. Obwohl es relativ wenig vom Baukörper zeigt, gibt es dem Betrachter auf einen Blick Auskunft über Funktion und Standort des Bauwerks: Es handelt sich eindeutig um die Bergstation einer Seilbahn, um die architektonische Hülle einer technischen Infrastruktur. Eindeutigkeit und klare Information sind nun einmal in Anbetracht der Fülle an visuellen Informationen mitentscheidend dafür, ob Aufmerksamkeit erlangt wird. Dazu kommt die spannungsvolle Bildkomposition, die sich etwa aus den verschiedenen, in der Bergstation fokussierenden Linien ergibt – die Stränge der Seilbahnseile, dazwischen der Berggipfel, darüber die Wolkenbänder.“

Claudia Wedekind, aut. architektur und tirol

"Unused. The main focus of this photograph is the jagged mountain landscape, the exposed location of the cable car station. The constructive elements, with their transparent membrane coverings, are shown with clarity. That the building is only partially visible means that the photograph is well adapted to supplementing others, for if one doesn't know the building, one might wonder – especially considering the leap of scale between the craggy landscape in the foreground and the cable car station in the background – exactly what function is actually performed by this object, hidden between boulders."

Most used. That this photograph of a mountain station of the Gaislachkogl Railway is the most-used one hardly surprises me, since we, too, have selected it as an 'image photo' a number of times. Although it reveals relatively little of the building's structure, it does tell us much about its function and location at a glance. Clearly this is the mountain station of a cable car railway, the architectonic shell of the technical infrastructure. Given the wealth of visual information, it is the presence of unambiguous, lucid information that determines whether the viewer's attention is elicited by the image. Then there is the taut composition, to some extent a result of the various lines that converge on the station – the clusters of cables that frame the peak of a mountain, topped by banks of clouds."

Claudia Wedekind, aut. architektur und tirol

Foto Photo Markus Bstieler, 2011
Architektur Architecture obermoser arch-omo
Projekt Project Seilbahn Cable car railway Gaislachkogl,
Sölden (AT), 2010

Foto Photo Markus Bstieler, 2013

Architektur Architecture bernardo bader architekten

Projekt Project Islamischer Friedhof Islamic cemetery,
Altach (AT), 2012

„Emblematische Bauten verlangen nach emblematischer Fotografie: Beim islamischen Friedhof in Altach ist es dem Architekten gelungen, einen bestimmten Ritus der Totenbestattung in Form zu gießen. Das Gebäude wird zum Emblem. Darin überlagern sich zwei Konzepte: das einer traditionell geprägten Glaubensrichtung mit der einer aufgeschlossenen, zeitgenössischen Architektursprache. Die meistgenutzte Fotografie verdeutlicht das auf einen Blick, selbst wenn sie sehr klein reproduziert wird. Sie verdichtet den Raum in der Nahaufnahme und gibt das Wesen der Anlage preis, die poetische Atmosphäre der Annäherung zweier Kulturen – Orient und Okzident. Sie wird selbst zum Emblem. Die Landschaftsaufnahme hingegen liefert den Kontext, zeichnet ein Bild der Region, in die das Gebäude eingebettet ist und verweist auf Größenordnungen. Der Inhalt kann nicht in der Deutlichkeit entschlüsselt werden."

Marina Hämmerle, Architektin und Architekturvermittlerin

"Emblematic buildings call for emblematic photographs. With the Islamic Cemetery in Altach, the architects have succeeded in articulating a form for a specific burial ritual. The building becomes an emblem. Two concepts are superimposed, that is, a traditional religious orientation and a receptive, contemporary architectural idiom. The most-used photograph provides clarity at a glance even when it is reproduced in quite small dimensions. It condenses the atmosphere in a close-up and discloses the essence of the facility, the poetic atmosphere where two cultures converge, East and West. It becomes an emblem in itself. The landscape photograph, on the other hand, supplies context, sketching an image of the terrain in which the building is embedded, referring to scale. The content cannot be explicitly decoded."

Marina Hämmerle, architect and architectural journalist

Foto Photo Rupert Steiner, 2000
Architektur Architecture Ortner & Ortner Baukunst
Projekt Project Museum Moderner Kunst,
Wien (AT), 2001

Foto Photo Rupert Steiner, 2001
Architektur Architecture Ortner & Ortner Baukunst
Projekt Project Museum Moderner Kunst,
Wien (AT), 2001

„In analogen Zeiten gab die Standardgröße des Leuchttisches und damit die Maximalanzahl der darauf zu platzierenden Ektachrome ein harmonisches Maß für die Bebilderung eines Architekturartikels vor. Die wahre Geschichte eines Projekts sollte im Zusammenspiel von Text und Bild erzählt werden. Das hat sich auch mit der digitalen Bilderflut und unter geänderten Abläufen mit den Werkzeugen der neuen Medien nicht geändert. Standardansichten sind zur Situierung unvermeidlich, doch ähnlich wie bei der Schönheit gibt auch hier erst die kleine, irritierende Abweichung von der Norm Aufschluss über und Einsicht in Idee und Umsetzung. Wir müssen hier mindestens diese beiden Fotos zeigen!"

Gerald A. Rödler, *architektur.aktuell*

"In analog times, the standard size of the light table, and hence the maximum number of Ektachromes that could be placed on it, prescribed a harmonious scale for the illustration of an architectural article. The project's real story had to be narrated via the interplay of text and image. Even with the flood of digital imagery and altered procedures using new equipment and media, this hasn't changed. To situate the architecture, standard views are indispensable, but as with beauty, it is the minimal, irritating deviation from the norm that provides information about the idea and its realization. Here, we must show at least these two photos!"

Gerald A. Rödler, *architektur.aktuell*

Foto Photo Markus Kaiser, 2011
Architektur Architecture Hermann Eisenköck,
Architektur Consult
Projekt Project Poolhaus Pool house Bullmann,
Ratsch an der Weinstraße (AT), 2010

Foto Photo Dietmar Tollerian/Archipicture, 2008
Architektur Architecture Kaufmann & Partner
Architekten
Projekt Project Power Tower – Energie AG Konzern-
zentrale Corporate headquarters, Linz (AT), 2008

Linke Seite: „Zum ersten Bild: Bildkompositorisch ist dies das spannendere Bild. Es kommt meist nicht zum Zug, weil nicht genug vom Turm zu sehen ist. Auch die extreme Perspektive führt manchmal zu Irritationen: ‚Ich wusste gar nicht, dass das Dach schräg ist!' Es ist der ungewohnte Blick aus der Nebenstraße. Nicht selten wird das Bild zum Quadrat beschnitten und der dunkle Vordergrund der Straße reduziert – das Gebäude wirkt dann nochmals gedrungener.

Zum zweiten Bild: Dies ist das Repräsentationsbild für das Projekt, das kollektiv verankerte Bild. Wahrscheinlich, weil es am besten zeigt, was das Projekt ausstrahlen sollte: Selbstbewusstsein, Eleganz, Licht, Energie. Manchmal wird das Bild rechts beschnitten; dann verliert es nicht nur die schwebende Laterne, sondern auch an Spannung. Ich habe oft versucht, den Blauton des Bildes in der Realität zu sehen. Es gibt ihn so nicht. Vielleicht ist auch das ein Grund, warum sich das Bild so einprägt: weil es eben doch nicht ganz die Wirklichkeit zeigt."

Mathias Haas, Kaufmann & Partner Architekten

Left page: "On the first image, compositionally, this is the more exciting picture. Usually it doesn't get a chance because too little of the tower is visible. Moreover, the extreme perspective sometimes causes annoyance such as, 'I didn't know the roof was slanted!' It shows an unfamiliar view from a side street. Sometimes this image is trimmed down to a square format, and the dark foreground of the street is reduced – then the building appears squatter.

On the second image, this is the representative picture for the project, the collectively anchored image. Probably because it shows best what the project was to have conveyed, i.e., self-confidence, elegance, light, energy. Sometimes this image is trimmed on the right and it loses not only the hovering streetlight but also its tension. I have often attempted to see the blue tone of this image in reality. It doesn't really exist. Perhaps that's one reason why this image is so memorable. It shows something that is not entirely real."

Mathias Haas, Kaufmann & Partner Architekten

Foto **Photo** Dietmar Tollerian / Archipicture, 2013
Architektur **Architecture** Wolf Architektur
Projekt **Project** Museum Angerlehner,
Thalheim (AT), 2013

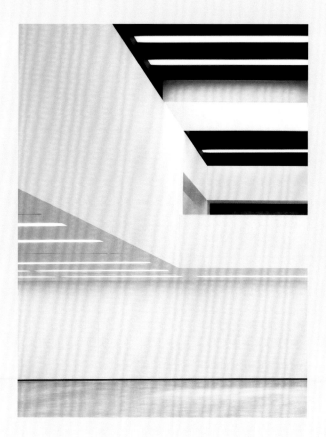

Foto Photo Bruno Klomfar, 2006
Architektur Architecture Dietrich | Untertrifaller
Architekten
Projekt Project Festspielhaus Festival hall,
Bregenz (AT), 2006

Foto **Photo** Paul Ott, 2006
Architektur **Architecture** Grabner/SPLITTERWERK
Projekt **Project** Orangerie d'Or, Graz (AT), 2005

„Architektur ist ein komplexes Phänomen, das Resultat vieler Überlegungen, Bedingungen, Dialoge, Entscheidungen. Doch vor Ort ist sie sofort zu begreifen. Dasselbe gilt für ein gutes Foto. Es vermittelt ein Gefühl für die Architektur und bringt vieles auf den Punkt. Mit dem ersten Blick folgt das Auge dem roten Teppich der gewendelten Treppe. Jeder weitere lässt mehr erkennen. Eine Ahnung vom städtebaulichen Kontext, der Nachbarschaft und Position des Raumes. Frei geformte Elemente feiern die Kultur und treffen auf Notwendigkeiten: Beton, Stahl, abgehängte Decken, Lüftungsrohre. Die Schatten am Boden verweisen auf die Glasfassade. Eine Idee von Form, Dimension, Funktion, Rhythmus und Bewegung entsteht, und eine Reflexion über das Fotografieren. Das erste Bild feiert stärker die Form und lädt das Auge zum Schweifen über Licht, Schatten, Atmosphäre, Farbigkeit und Materialität ein: gerade, rund, hell, dunkel, glänzend, matt. Nähe, Distanz. Es redet anders vom selben Raum, abstrakter. Auch wahr.“

Isabella Marboe, Architekturjournalistin, Redakteurin *architektur.aktuell*

"Architecture is a complex phenomenon, the result of numerous considerations, conditions, dialogs, decisions. Yet on site, it becomes immediately graspable. The same is true of a good photograph. It conveys a feeling for the architecture and encapsulates a great deal. At first glance, the eye follows the red carpet on the spiral staircase. Each subsequent glance reveals more, a hint, for example, of the urban context, of neighboring structures and position in space. Freely formed elements celebrate culture and run up against inescapable realities: concrete, steel, suspended ceilings, ventilation ducts. The shadows on the floor allude to the glass facade. There emerges an idea of form, dimension, function, rhythm, and movement, and a reflection on the photographic. The first image celebrates form more emphatically, inviting the eye to roam through light, shadow, atmosphere, color, and materiality: straight, round, bright, dark, glossy, matt. Near, distant. It speaks differently of the same space, more abstractly. But also truthfully."

Isabella Marboe, architectural journalist, editor of *architektur.aktuell*

Foto **Photo** Pez Hejduk, 2009
Architektur **Architecture** Ben van Berkel – UNStudio
Projekt **Project** MUMUTH – Haus für Musik und
Musiktheater **House of music and musical theatre,**
Graz (AT), 2008

75

Von Menschen und Räumen
Of People and Spaces

: Nutzungsbeziehungen
: Relations of Use

In den letzten Jahren wurde häufig kritisiert, dass Bauwerke in Architekturzeitschriften meist menschenleer gezeigt werden. Fassaden wirken unbelebt, Wohnzimmer perfekt, aber steril. Kein Leben kreuzt den architektonischen Plan. Doch wie die folgenden Seiten zeigen, verharrt die Architekturfotografie keineswegs im Paradigma der Abstraktion von Funktion. Diese Bilder widmen sich ganz der Schnittstelle von Mensch und Raum. Das beginnt bei den Bauarbeitern: Welche Beziehung haben sie zur Architektur, die unter ihren Händen entsteht? Bereits kleine Spuren – eine bestimmte Anordnung von Gegenständen im Raum wie ein Paar Hausschuhe neben einem Schreibtisch oder herumliegendes Spielzeug – geben aufschlussreiche Einblicke in individuelle Lebenswelten. Manchmal tauchen Nutzerinnen und Nutzer nur schemenhaft auf, versunken, ganz bei sich. Anderswo glaubt man, in Fluren und auf Stegen Kinderlachen zu hören. Inszenierte Portraits bringen kulturelle Vorbilder zum Vorschein oder verraten intime Träume.

Es gibt Ausstellungsarchitekturen, die Besucherinnen und Besucher brauchen, um komplett zu werden, und es gibt ehemalige Privathäuser, die durch die Publikumsströme zu ausgestellten Ikonen werden. Auf Fotografien gelingt es, Dinge und Menschen gleichberechtigt zu versammeln, wenn sie in der Weite eines Platzes in Dialog treten, vereint durch die dramatischen Schatten der tief stehenden Sonne, oder wenn sich Wiener Würstel, Kebab und Falafel in der Dämmerung treffen. Wessen Schachteln lagern in einem Hof in Shenzhen und wer wohnt wohl in einem Haus von Jean Nouvel in Mulhouse? Penibel aufgeräumt wirkt eine Obdachlosenunterkunft in Tokio, die Schuhe fein säuberlich vor der behelfsmäßigen Tür abgestellt. Der Bordstein wird zum Garten. Gibt es sogar ein Haustier? Weit über die Repräsentation von Architektur hinaus erzählen die Fotografinnen und Fotografen ihre eigenen Geschichten, stets respektvoll, nahe an den Menschen, aber nie voyeuristisch. AF

In recent years the objection has often been raised that buildings are illustrated in architectural magazines as if they were devoid of people. Facades seem deserted, living rooms immaculate but sterile. No life forms intersect with the architectural design. But as we learn in the following pages, architectural photography by no means remains within the paradigm of abstraction from function. These images are wholly devoted to the interface between the human individual and architectural space. This begins with construction workers. What is their relationship to the architecture that emerges through their labor? Even the smallest hints – a certain arrangement of objects in space, such as a pair of slippers alongside a desk, a toy left lying on the floor – can provide telling insights into individual life worlds. At times, users are visible only as shadowy figures, wholly self-absorbed. Elsewhere, in corridors or on arcades, you can almost hear the laughter of children. Staged portraits bring cultural models to the surface or else reveal the most intimate dreams.

Certain works of exhibition architecture require the visitor's presence to become complete, and some former private homes become display icons through the flow of visitors. In photographs, it becomes possible to assemble objects and people on equal terms, i.e., when they enter into dialog on the broad expanse of a plaza, joined by the dramatic shadows of the setting sun, or when Viennese sausage, kebab, and falafel meet in the twilight. Whose boxes are stored in a courtyard in Shenzhen, and who might live in a house built by Jean Nouvel in Mulhouse? A homeless shelter in Tokyo makes an impression of fastidious tidiness, the shoes arranged neatly in front of a makeshift door. The sidewalk becomes a front garden. Perhaps there is even a pet? Far beyond representations of architecture, these photographers narrate their own stories, consistently respectful, close to the realities of human existence, never voyeuristic. AF

Foto **Photo** Angelo Kaunat, 2000
Architektur **Architecture** Ortner & Ortner Baukunst
Projekt **Project** Kunsthalle Wien, Museumsquartier,
Wien (AT), 2001

Foto Photo Manfred Seidl, 2010
Architektur Architecture ARTEC Architekten,
Bettina Götz + Richard Manahl
Projekt Project Wohnbau Housing estate Tokiostraße,
Die Bremer Stadtmusikanten, Wien (AT), 2009

79

Foto Photo Lukas Schaller, 2005
Architektur Architecture Ateliers Jean Nouvel,
Duncan Lewis / Hervé Potin / BLOCK Architectes
Projekt Project Cité Manifeste, Muhlhouse (FR), 2005

Foto **Photo** Peter Eder, 1995
Architektur **Architecture** Frank Lloyd Wright
Projekt **Project** Fallingwater, Bear Run (US), 1938

Foto Photo Peter Eder, 2008

Architektur Architecture HoG architektur

Projekt Project 4 Marktplätze im oststeirischen

Hügelland 4 market squares in the hill country of eastern

Styria, St. Margarethen an der Raab (AT), 2008

Foto **Photo** Rupert Steiner, Gänsehäufel,
aus der Serie from the series Transdanubien,
Wien (AT), 1996

Foto **Photo** Dietmar Tollerian/Archipicture, 2012
Architektur **Architecture** Kaufmann & Partner
Architekten
Projekt **Project** City Center One Zagreb East,
Zagreb (HR), 2012

Foto **Photo** Rupert Steiner, 2002
Künstler **Artist** Ugo Rondinone
Ausstellung **Exhibition** No How On, kuratiert von
curated by Gerald Matt, Kunsthalle Wien,
Wien (AT), 2002
Architektur **Architecture** Ortner & Ortner
Baukunst, 2001

Foto **Photo** Dietmar Tollerian/Archipicture, 2006
Ausstellungsansicht **Exhibition view** Museen im
21. Jahrhundert (**Museums in the 21st century**)
Konzept **concept** Suzanne Greub, Thierry Greub,
Art Centre Basel
Ausstellungsarchitektur **Exhibition architecture**
caramel architekten, LENTOS Kunstmuseum Linz,
Linz (AT), 2006
Architektur **Architecture** Weber Hofer Partner
Architekten, 2003

Foto **Photo** Pia Odorizzi, 1999

Architektur **Architecture** Karl Odorizzi

Projekt **Project** Wohnlandschaft mit Hallenbad

Living space with indoor swimming pool,

Marchtrenk (AT), 1999

Foto Photo Stefan Oláh, 15., Neubaugürtel,
Wien (AT), aus from Fünfundneunzig Wiener
Würstelstände – The Hot 95, 2011

Foto **Photo** Angelo Kaunat, 1997

Architektur **Architecture** Peter Zumthor

Projekt **Project** Kunsthaus Bregenz, Bregenz (AT), 1997

Foto Photo Manfred Seidl, 2010
Architektur Architecture Geiswinkler & Geiswinkler
Projekt Project Karrée Block St. Marx,
Wien (AT), 2010

Foto Photo Günter Richard Wett, 2011
Architektur Architecture LAAC Architekten,
Stiefel Kramer Architecture
Projekt Project Landhausplatz, Eduard Wallnöfer
Platz, Innsbruck (AT), 2010

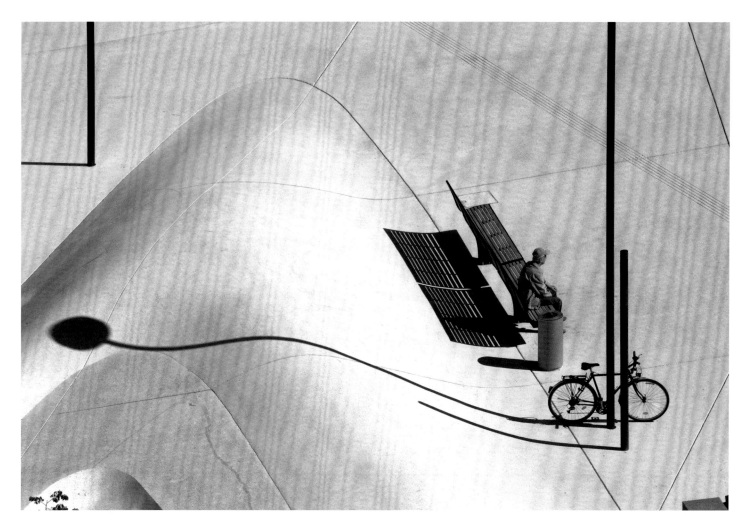

Foto Photo Margherita Spiluttini, 1999

Architektur Architecture BKK Architekten

Projekt Project Wohnhausanlage Housing complex

Sargfabrik, Badehaus Bathhouse, Wien (AT), 1996

Foto Photo Stefan Oláh, aus from Österreichische
Architektur der Fünfziger Jahre (Austrian Architecture
of the 1950s), 2011
Architektur Architecture Karl Hütter
Projekt Project Schneidersalon Tailor shop
Bernschütz, Wien (AT), 1958

Foto Photo Paul Ott, TOD DEM ARCHITEKT
(Death to the architect), Graz (AT), 1995

Foto Photo Zita Oberwalder, 2015
Projekt Project Titanic Dock, Belfast (UK)

Foto Photo Zita Oberwalder, 2010
Architektur Architecture Juan Batanero
Projekt Project La Salve Brücke Bridge,
Bilbao (ES), 1972
Künstler Artist Daniel Buren
Projekt Project Arcos rojos, 2007

Foto Photo Günter Richard Wett, aus from
Spurensuche in Brasilien (Searching for traces in Brazil) –
Artigas, Bo Bardi, Mendes da Rocha, 2008
Architektur Architecture Lina Bo Bardi
Projekt Project SESC Fábrica Pompéia, Umnutzung
einer Fabrikanlage zu einem Kultur- und Sport-
zentrum Conversion of a factory into a cultural and sports
center, São Paulo (BR), 1986

Foto Photo Markus Kaiser, 2013
Architektur Architecture Zaha Hadid Architects
Projekt Project Library and Learning Centre,
Wirtschaftsuniversität Wien Vienna University of
Economics and Business, Wien (AT), 2013

Foto Photo Peter Eder, 2008
Architektur Architecture LPS – Leitner Pretterhofer
Simbeni
Projekt Project Sportzentrum Sports Center,
Dobl (AT), 2008

Foto Photo Gisela Erlacher, Jiulongpo,
Chongqing (RC), 2011

Foto Photo Hertha Hurnaus, Franz West fotografiert
in seinem Wiener Atelier Franz West in his Vienna studio
für den Katalog for the catalog Sammlung West, 1995
Künstler Artist (Wand wall) Martin Kippenberger

Foto Photo Hertha Hurnaus, aus der Serie from the
series Homeless Architecture Tokyo,
Tokio (JP), 2004

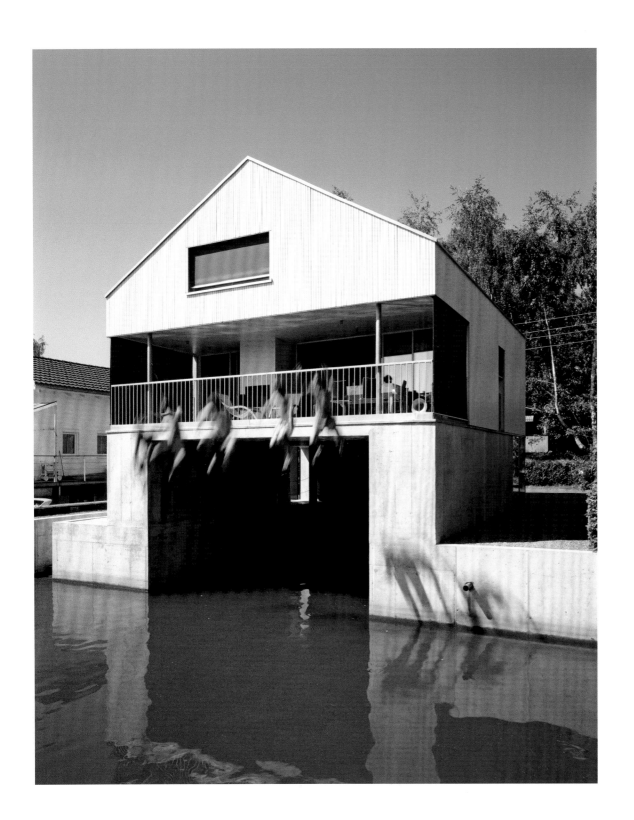

Foto Photo Bruno Klomfar, 2004
Architektur Architecture wolfgang ritsch
baukunst
Projekt Project Haus M, Fußach (AT), 2004

Foto **Photo** Bruno Klomfar, 2012
Architektur **Architecture** Dietrich | Untertrifaller
Architekten
Projekt **Project** Haus **House** SF, Dornbirn (AT), 2012

Foto **Photo** Stefan Oláh, aus **from** Museumsdepots –
Inside the Museum Storage, Wien (AT), 2012

Von Räumen und Menschen: Nutzungsbeziehungen

Foto **Photo** Günter Richard Wett, aus **from**
Spurensuche in Brasilien (**Searching for traces in Brazil**) –
Artigas, Bo Bardi, Mendes da Rocha, 2008
Architektur **Architecture** Vilanova Artigas,
Carlos Cascaldi
Projekt **Project** FAU USP – Faculdade de Arquite-
tura e Urbanismo da Universidade de São Paulo,
São Paulo (BR), 1965

Sichtwechsel
Shift of Perspective

: Vom Nutzen des Standpunkts
: On the Use of Viewpoint

Fotoaufträge werden meist vorab besprochen: Was ist die Leitidee des Projekts? Was soll gezeigt, kommuniziert werden und was vielleicht eher nicht? Aber wie jeder Beobachter hat auch jeder Urheber eines Gebäudes oder einer Publikation einen blinden Fleck. In den beauftragten Fotos können überraschend Dinge zu Tage treten, die ganz anders geplant waren oder zumindest im Prozess des Entwurfs nicht bewusst mitgedacht wurden: Der architektonisch inszenierte Blick auf die schöne Landschaft wird von einer alternativen Perspektive auf den baulichen Wildwuchs der direkten Nachbarschaft unterlaufen. Das spektakuläre Bankgebäude fügt sich auf erstaunliche Weise in die Zweckbauten der Umgebung. Der klar abgegrenzte Sichtbetonkubus eines Zubaus verschmilzt unter den Schneemassen mit dem denkmalgeschützten Bestand.

Die Fotografie kann die Absicht der Architektur verstärken, die Leitidee eines Konzepts herausarbeiten und die Komplexität einer Herangehensweise in einem einzigen Bild verdichten: Ein Fiat Panda wird zum Hauptdarsteller der Erfolgsgeschichte zwischen Innovation und Alltag in einem kleinen italienischen Weinort. Am Semmering wird der Raum zwischen den Dingen zum Träger einer einzigartigen Kulturlandschaft. In den Tiroler Bergen versteckt sich das neue Festspielhaus in der Dämmerung, lässt dem Bestandsbau seinen Auftritt, um auf den zweiten Blick umso spektakulärer hervorzutreten. Die Standpunkte der Fotografinnen und Fotografen eröffnen den Auftraggebern eine Schleife der Selbstreflexion. So wird aus einem Auftragsverhältnis eine echte Zusammenarbeit. AF

For the most part, photo commissions are discussed beforehand. What is the project's guiding idea? What is to be shown, conveyed, and what perhaps withheld? But like every observer, every author of a building or publication has a blind spot. In the commissioned photos, astonishing things may come to light, things planned entirely differently – or at least never consciously intended – during the design process. An architecturally staged prospect of a beautiful landscape, for example, is undermined by an alternative view that reveals uncontrolled growth in the immediate vicinity. A spectacular bank building adapts itself in astonishing ways to the surrounding utilitarian structures. Under masses of snow, the clearly delimited, exposed concrete cube of an extension merges with the pre-existing landmarks-protected architectural inventory.

Photography is capable of heightening the intention of the architecture, clarifying its guiding idea, condensing the complexity of a design strategy into a single image. Thus, a Fiat Panda becomes the lead actor in a success story between innovation and everyday life in a small Italian winegrowing locale. In Semmering, the space between objects becomes the medium of a singular cultural landscape. In the Tyrolean Mountains, the new festival theater hides in the twilight, allowing the pre-existing development to make an entrance, and hence seems all the more spectacular at second glance. The photographer's point of view opens up a circuit of self-reflection for the client. In this way, a contractual relationship becomes a genuine collaboration. AF

Foto Photo Hertha Hurnaus, 2005

Architektur Architecture Vladimír Dedeček

Projekt Project Slowakisches Nationalarchiv

Slovakian National Archives, Bratislava (SK),1983

Foto Photo Hertha Hurnaus, Fotoessay photo-essay
aus from Harry Glück. Wohnbauten,
Hg. ed. Reinhard Seiß, Müry Salzmann Verlag, 2013
Architektur Architecture Harry Glück, Kurt Hlaweniczka,
Requat & Reinthaller & Partner Architekten
Projekt Project Wohnpark Residential park Alt Erlaa,
Wien (AT), 1985

Foto Photo Gisela Erlacher, Freyung,
Wien (AT), 2011

„Le Corbusier verwendete für die Fotografien seiner Gebäude zeitgenössische Automobile, um die Gebäude als futuristische Wohnmaschinen mit deren Technologie gleichzusetzen. Heute wirken diese Autos unendlich alt und die Gebäude noch immer aktuell. Auf Fotos von Rem Koolhaas' Maison à Bordeaux sind alte Alfa Romeos und Citroëns zu sehen, die die Distinguiertheit der Bauherren verdeutlichen. Hertha Hurnaus gelingt es, mit Giorgetto Giugiaros Meisterwerk Fiat Panda das Winecenter gekonnt, aber beiläufig in Szene zu setzen und einen für unsere Arbeit zentralen kulturanthropologischen Bezug zum Alltag zu vermitteln: Die kleine Ikone des italienischen Alltags, im Wechselspiel zwischen Nonkonformismus und Pragmatismus, hier in gewagtem Türkis als Statement gegen die Eintönigkeit. Sie verortet das Gebäude im ländlichen Raum und im italienischen Kontext, stellt den Bezug zu den Auftraggebern her und wirft nicht zuletzt die Frage nach der Zeitlosigkeit guten Designs auf."

Michael Obrist, feld72

"For photographs of his buildings, Le Corbusier used contemporary automobiles, identifying his houses – futuristic machines for living – with their technology. Today these cars seem infinitely old, while the buildings still seem contemporary. Old Alfa Romeos and Citroëns are visible in photographs of Rem Koolhaas's Maison à Bordeaux, which attest the owners' distinction. With Giorgetto Giugiaro's masterpiece, the Fiat Panda, Hertha Hurnaus skillfully yet casually places the Wine Center in a setting, conveying a cultural-anthropological reference to the everyday that is central to our work, i.e., a little icon of everyday Italian life, an interplay between nonconformism and pragmatism, here in bold turquoise as a protest against monotony. She situates the building in rural areas and in the Italian context, establishing a reference to the client, and not least of all, poses the question of the timelessness of good design."

Michael Obrist, feld72

Foto Photo Hertha Hurnaus, 2006
Architektur Architecture feld72
Projekt Project Winecenter & Raika, Kaltern (IT), 2006

Foto **Photo** Alexander Eugen Koller, 2002
Architektur **Architecture** Söhne & Partner Architekten
Projekt **Project** Babenberger Passage, Wien (AT), 2002

„Das Bild gefällt uns deshalb so gut, weil es vieldeutig ist. Zum einen ist es eine zweidimensionale, abstrakte Darstellung, ähnlich einem Gemälde oder einer Grafik. Bei längerer Betrachtung gewinnt es allerdings an Tiefe, wird durch die Darstellung der Treppe und des Zylinders dreidimensional. Diese Mehrdeutigkeit wird durch die Abbildung des Spiegels noch verstärkt. Er täuscht einen zusätzlichen Raum vor und verwischt damit noch stärker die Grenzen zwischen den Welten. Genau dieses Hinterfragen und Verwischen von Dimensionen bringt die ursprüngliche Idee des Entwurfs für die Babenberger Passage wieder hervor und setzt sie bewusst in Szene."

Söhne & Partner Architekten

"This image appeals to us so forcefully because it is ambiguous. On the one hand, it is two-dimensional, abstract, like a painting or a print. Upon closer examination, however, it acquires depth, becomes three-dimensional by virtue of its depiction of the staircase and the cylinder. This equivocal quality is heightened by the presence of the mirror. This creates the illusion of an additional space, erasing the boundary between worlds even more emphatically. Precisely this questioning and blurring of dimensions reproduces the original idea of the design for the Babenberger Passage, consciously lending its presentation a carefully staged aspect."

Söhne & Partner Architekten

„Der Blick des Fotografen als Dokument wandelbarer Architektur durch den Einfluss natürlicher Phänomene."

Hanno Schlögl, Architekt

"The gaze of the photographer as a document of architecture that changes through the influence of natural phenomena."

Hanno Schlögl, architect

Foto Photo Markus Bstieler, 2008
Architektur Architecture Schlögl & Süß Architekten
(2006); Franz Baumann (1928)
Projekt Project Innsbrucker Nordkettenbahnen Neu,
Innsbruck (AT), 2006

Foto Photo Pez Hejduk, 1999
Architektur Architecture Raimund Dickinger
Projekt Project Werkhalle Orgelbau Walter Vonbank

Workshop of the organ builder Walter Vonbank,
Triebendorf (AT), 1996

Sichtwechsel: Vom Nutzen des Standpunkts

Foto **Photo** Margherita Spiluttini, 1999
Architektur **Architecture** Henke Schreieck
Architekten
Projekt **Project** Terrassenhaus **Split-level house**
Seefeld, Seefeld (AT), 1995

„Unsere Intention war, mit den geschlossenen Terrassenbrüstungen den touristischen Wildwuchs des Ortes auszublenden, um den Blick auf die ‚schöne' Landschaft zu fokussieren. Margherita Spiluttini hat mit ihrem Blick die ‚wahre' Landschaft ins Bild gerückt."

Henke Schreieck Architekten

"Our intention was to use the closed terrace balustrades to block out the uncontrolled touristic growth of the locale, guiding the eye to the 'beautiful' landscape. With her point of view, Margherita Spiluttini shifted the 'true' landscape into view."

Henke Schreieck Architekten

„Die ursprüngliche Idee für die Bildserie Stadtbahnbogen war, verschiedenste architektonische Lösungen zur Schließung einer Arkade anhand von Frontalaufnahmen zu präsentieren. Stefan Oláh hat durch die Variation von Perspektive und Abstand sowie die Einbeziehung der räumlichen Umgebung, des Himmelsausschnitts und der jahreszeitlichen Atmosphäre eine stärker stadttopografische Arbeit daraus gemacht; die Arkaden haben an Individualität gewonnen. Oláhs Arbeitsweise mit Fachkamera, analogem Aufnahmematerial und lithografischer Nachbearbeitung führt tendenziell zu einer Heroisierung des Dargestellten, das Allgemeingültigkeit beansprucht. Gleichzeitig – und das ist das Dialektische daran – zeigt sich eine gewisse ironische Distanz zum Bildinhalt."

Andreas Lehne, Kunsthistoriker

"The original idea for a series of images of commuter railway arches was to use straight-on images to present the most diverse architectural solutions to the closing of an arcade. By varying perspective and distance, and integrating the spatial surroundings, sections of the sky, and the seasonal atmosphere, Stefan Oláh creates a powerful work of urban topography; the arcades acquire individuality. Oláh's working approach with view camera, analog photographic material, and lithographic post-processing, tends to heroize what is depicted, raising claims to universality. Yet one can detect at the same time (and here is the dialectical aspect) a certain ironic distance in relation to the image content."

Andreas Lehne, art historian

Foto Photo Stefan Oláh, aus from Stadtbahnbogenˣ, 2012
Architektur Architecture Otto Wagner
Projekt Project Bogen Arch 238, Wien (AT), 1901

114

Sichtwechsel: Vom Nutzen des Standpunkts

Foto **Photo** Paul Ott, 2006
Architektur **Architecture** 4000architekten
Projekt **Project** Schanzenstraße Geb. 34 – 3,
Köln (DE), 2006

„Unbekannte Aspekte im eigenen Projekt? Gibt es nicht. Aber in einem Foto, das den Eingriff kaum zeigt, die Idee eben dieses Eingriffs – eine glatte Haut in alter Fabrik – zu zeigen, das ist großartig."

Georg Giebeler, 4000architekten

"Unknown aspects of one's own project? There are none. But to show the idea of an intervention in a photograph that barely shows the intervention itself – a smooth skin in an old factory – is really great."

Georg Giebeler, 4000architekten

Foto **Photo** Manfred Seidl, 2014
Architektur **Architecture** Geiswinkler & Geiswinkler
Projekt **Project** Wohnbau **Housing estate** Mautner
Markhof Gründe, Wien (AT), 2014

Sichtwechsel: Vom Nutzen des Standpunkts

Foto Photo Günter Richard Wett, 2014
Architektur Architecture Robert Schuller, 1959;
Delugan Meissl Associated Architects, 2012;
Kleboth Lindinger Dollnig KLD, 2013
Projekt Project Tiroler Festspiele Erl
Tyrolian festival Erl, Erl (AT)

„Der Raum als Hauptdarsteller in Gisela Erlachers Arbeiten verharrt im Augenblick der Fotografie und beginnt sodann mit der Erzählung des Ortes. Für sich stehend, ohne weiteren Kommentar, weisen uns ihre Fotografien auf gewöhnliche Details hin und erzählen in Abwesenheit von Akteurinnen oder Akteuren reiche Geschichten über das Unscheinbare."

Roland Tusch, Autor *Wächterhäuser an der Semmeringbahn*

"The space, as the lead actor in Gisela Erlacher's images, pauses in the instant of the exposure, thereby initiating a narrative of place. Standing for themselves, without further commentary, her photographs call attention to commonplace details, telling us, in the absence of human participants, rich tales of the inconspicuous."

Roland Tusch, author *Wächterhäuser an der Semmeringbahn*

Foto Photo Gisela Erlacher, aus from Fotoessay
Photographic essay, in: Roland Tusch, Wächterhäuser
an der Semmeringbahn, 2014

Foto **Photo** Lukas Schaller, 2007
Architektur **Architecture** Wolfgang Tschapeller
und **and** Wolfram Mehlem
Projekt **Project** Haus **House** St. Joseph,
St. Andrä-Wördern (AT), 2007
W. Tschapeller im Haus **inside the house** St. Joseph

„Wir haben das St. Josef Haus immer wieder fotografieren lassen: mit verschiedenen Kameras, von verschiedenen Fotografen, in verschiedenen Bauphasen, und obwohl es während des Fotografierens bereits Gebäude war, nicht mehr Plan und nicht mehr Modell, wirkte die Kamera wie eine Art Rückspiegel oder Filter, der das Gebäude wieder zum Modell machte."

Wolfgang Tschapeller, Architekt

"We had the House St. Josef photographed repeatedly, with various cameras, by various photographers, in various building phases, and although it was already a building when it was being photographed, no longer a floor plan and no longer a model, the camera functioned like a kind of rearview mirror or filter that converted the building back into a model."

Wolfgang Tschapeller, architect

Foto Photo Bruno Klomfar, 2010
Architektur Architecture Nägele Waibel,
wolfgang ritsch baukunst, Bruno Spagolla
Projekt Project Hafen Harbor, Bregenz (AT), 2010

Foto Photo Alexander Eugen Koller, 2014
Architektur Architecture Johann Ferdinand
Hetzendorf von Hohenberg
Projekt Project Schloss Schönbrunn, Großes
Parterre und Gloriette, Wien (AT), 1775

121

„Trotzdem und mit Freude: Ich habe nicht die Illusion, Fotografie könne die eigentliche Wirkung von Architektur und ihren Innenräumen vermitteln. Trotzdem ist die Fotografie das bedeutungsvollste Vermittlungsinstrument für unser Tun und wird zunehmend wichtiger, obwohl sie vom Wesentlichen ablenkt, das nur vor Ort erlebt werden kann. Fotografie ist Kunst, und mit der Auftragsarchitekturfotografie gerät sie in eine ‚Zwickmühle', die auch unsere eigene Arbeit kennzeichnet. Um parallel zu meinen Bauten ein homogenes ‚Bildwerk' entstehen zu lassen, beauftrage ich immer denselben Fotografen. Wir überraschen uns hin und wieder mit der Entdeckung von Kamerastandorten, und wir setzen uns über Licht, Wetter und die Morgenstunden auseinander. Ich erzähle von der inneren und äußeren raison d'être jedes Baus, verhandle nicht beim Honorar und freue mich über die Bilder."

Rainer Köberl, Architekt

Foto Photo Lukas Schaller, 2007
Architektur Architecture Rainer Köberl
Projekt Project Sensei – Sushibar zum Roten Fisch,
Innsbruck (AT), 2007
Rainer Köberl mit seinen Auftraggebern with his
clients Dil Ghamal und and Devta Ghamal

"Nevertheless and gladly, I have no illusion that photography can convey the genuine impact of architecture and its interiors. All the same, photography is the most important intermediary instrument for our activities and is becoming increasingly important – even though it distracts from the essential, which can only be experienced on site. Photography is an art, and through commissioned architectural photography it is prey to a dilemma, one that also characterizes our own work. In order to allow a homogenous 'image inventory' to emerge alongside my buildings, I always commission the same photographers. At times we are astonished with the discovery of camera positions, and we become preoccupied with light, weather conditions, the morning hour. I discuss the inner and outer raison d'être of each building, never bargain when it comes to fees, and am delighted with the pictures."

Rainer Köberl, architect

Foto **Photo** Lukas Schaller, 2011
Architektur **Architecture** Rainer Köberl
Projekt **Project** BTV – Bank für Tirol und
Vorarlberg, Zweigstelle Mitterweg,
Innsbruck (AT), 2011

„Schallers Fotografie vollbringt das Kunststück, die Bankfiliale in die Gebrauchsarchitektur der umliegenden Gebäude einzubetten, ohne beide miteinander gemein zu machen. Aus den Flachdachkästen ragt die Pyramide als originelles Anderes empor. Gleichzeitig findet ihre schachbrettartige Fassadengestaltung einen Widerhall im rot-weiß lackierten Rahmen eines Fußballtores und im Raster der Glasbausteine. Die Markierung des Tartanfelds komplettiert die Bildkomposition aus einfachen plani- und stereometrischen Formen: Kreis, Dreieck, Rechteck, Quadrat, Pyramide. Ihr wahres Pendant findet die BTV freilich in der erhabenen Natur. Wie zufällig reiht sich ihr First als höchster Gipfel in den Bergkamm der Nordkette ein."

Fabian Knierim, Kurator WestLicht. Schauplatz für Fotografie

"Schaller's photograph pulls off the feat of embedding the branch bank in the functional architecture of the surrounding buildings, yet without homogenizing them. The pyramid looms up out of the flat-roofed boxes like an original other. At the same time, its checkerboard-style facade design finds an echo in the red-and-white painted framework of a soccer goalpost and a grid of glass bricks. The markings of the Tartan track complete the picture, composed of simple planimetric and stereometric forms: circle, triangle, rectangle, square, pyramid. The BTV, of course, finds its real counterpart in the sublimity of nature. As though by chance, its roof ridge joins the Nordkette mountain range, now as its highest peak."

Fabian Knierim, curator of WestLicht. Schauplatz für Fotografie

Bühne

Stage

: Nutzungskontext
: Contexts of Use

Gebäude stehen nicht als Solitäre im leeren Raum. Sie müssen in ihrer Umgebung platziert werden, ob durch Abgrenzung oder durch Bezugnahmen. Besonders interessant wird es, wenn sich Architektur nicht nur verortet, sondern einen Ort schafft. Wie aber vermittelt ein Foto die Seele eines Ortes? Indem alt und neu gleichberechtigt zueinander finden oder indem sie, ganz im Gegenteil, in einen vehementen Maßstabskonflikt treten? Vorhandenes und Neues können sich in den Reflexionen einer Glasfassade vermischen. Hinzugefügtes kann natürlicher wirken als die vorhandene Kulturlandschaft. Manchmal fällt es schwer, das eigentliche Sujet zu erraten: Ist es die Tankstelle oder sind es die Hochhäuser dahinter, ist es der gründerzeitliche Prunkbau oder der Würstelstand am Eck, die Verkehrstrasse oder der Häuserblock, sind es die Vergnügungsdampfer oder ist es das Opernhaus an der Küste? Stehlen die Berge dem Bauwerk die Show? Wird die Dachterrasse im Stadtpanorama zur Nebendarstellerin? Mit der Entscheidung, ob ein Gebäude das Bild dominiert oder im Spiel von Figur und Hintergrund fast zum Verschwinden gebracht wird, intensivieren die Fotografinnen und Fotografen die Beziehung von Ort und Architektur. Sie zeigen, dass der Kontext den Unterschied macht, sei es der landschaftliche oder der gebaute, die beide immer auch ökonomische und politische Kontexte sind.

Gleichzeitig werden auch die Fotos selbst durch ihren visuellen Kontext beeinflusst. Ob fette Headlines, Bildunterschriften oder korrespondierende Textspalten, sie alle verändern die Wirkung der Bilder. Ein Architekturfoto hat viele Leben, in vielen Auflösungen, Farbigkeiten und Kontexten. Das gilt umso mehr, wenn ein Foto die Printmedien verlässt und als raumüberspannender Baldachin auftritt oder in den winzigen Projektionskammern eines Diabetrachters verschwindet. AF

Buildings do not stand around like solitary objects in empty space. They must be positioned within their surroundings, whether by being delimited from it or by referring to it. Particularly interesting are cases where a work of architecture is not merely situated within a place but actually creates one. But how does a photograph convey the spirit of the place? By allowing old and new to find common ground on equal terms, or by allowing them to enact a vehement conflict between contrasting criteria? In the reflections of a glazed facade, pre-existing and new can mingle. That which has been added may seem more natural than the pre-existing cultural landscape. At times it is difficult to define the actual subject. Is it the gas station or the high rise behind it? The splendid Wilhelminian-era building or the sausage stand on the corner? The thoroughfare or the block of buildings? The pleasure cruiser or the opera house on the coastline? Do the mountains steal the limelight from the architecture? Does the roof terrace become a supporting actor within the urban panorama? When deciding whether a building is to dominate an image or instead to virtually disappear into the interplay of figure and ground, photographers intensify the relationship between architecture and place. They demonstrate how the context makes all the difference, whether landscape or constructed, and that both are always economic and political in character as well.

At the same time, the photographs themselves are influenced by their visual contexts. Whether bold-printed headlines, captions, or related columns of text, all alter an image's impact. An architectural photograph has many lives in many degrees of resolution, color schemes, and contexts. This is all the more true when a photograph exits print media to appear as a space-spanning canopy, or disappears into the tiny dimensions of a slide viewer. AF

Foto **Photo** Lukas Schaller, Cité du Londeau,
Noisy-le-Sec, Bobigny (FR), 2005

Foto **Photo** Dietmar Tollerian/Archipicture,
aus **from** Kirchenbau nach 1945 (**Church buildings
after 1945**), Diözese Linz, 2003
Architektur **Architecture** Franz Wiesmayr
Projekt **Project** St. Severin, Linz (AT), 1968

Foto Photo Angelo Kaunat, 1997
Architektur Architecture Dani Freixes,
Varis Arquitectes
Projekt Project Facultat de Ciènces de la
Comunicació, Barcelona (ES), 1996

128

Foto Photo Paul Ott, 2005
Ausstellungsarchitektur Exhibition architecture
SPLITTERWERK, AS-IF
Ausstellung Exhibition Ornament & Display,
kuratiert von curated by Angelika Fitz,
kunsthaus mürz, Mürzzuschlag (AT), 2005
Architektur Architecture Konrad Frey, 1991

Foto **Photo** Hertha Hurnaus, aus der Ausstellung
from the exhibition Out of Context, Galerie Prisma,
Bozen (IT), 2008
Architektur **Architecture** AllesWirdGut
Projekt **Project** Open Air Festspielarena im
Römersteinbruch **Open air festival arena at the Roman**
Quarry, St. Margarethen (AT), 2008

130

Foto **Photo** Pez Hejduk, 2014
Architektur **Architecture** BIG – Bjarke Ingels Group
Projekt **Project** Wohnhausanlage **Housing estate**
The Mountain Dwellings, Kopenhagen (DK), 2008

Foto Photo Bruno Klomfar, 2011

Architektur Architecture Theophil Hansen

Projekt Project Parlament Parliament building, Wien (AT), 1883

Installation Installation proHolz Austria – Tag des Waldes

Day of forests, 2011

132

Foto **Photo** Bruno Klomfar, 2008
Architektur **Architecture** Dietrich | Untertrifaller Architekten
Projekt **Project** Ausstellung **Exhibition** Rural Urbanism,
Galerie Aedes, Berlin (DE), 2008

Foto Photo Markus Kaiser, 2013
Architektur Architecture COOP HIMMELB(L)AU;
Karl Schwanzer
Projekt Project BMW Welt, 2007;
BMW-Vierzylinder, 1973, München (DE)

134

Foto **Photo** Angelo Kaunat, 2012
Architektur **Architecture** kadawittfeldarchitektur
Projekt **Project** Salzburger Hauptbahnhof
Salzburg main railway station, Salzburg (AT), 2014

Foto **Photo** Stefan Oláh, APOLLO Garage,
Apollogasse 11–13, Wien (AT), aus **from**
Sechsundzwanzig Wiener Tankstellen, 2009

136

Foto Photo Pez Hejduk, 2011
Architektur Architecture Otto Prutscher
Projekt Project Koptisch-orthodoxe Kirche
St. Markus, Wien (AT), 1917
Architektur Architecture Johann Staber
Projekt Project Vienna International Centre,
Wien (AT), 1979

Foto Photo Eduard Hueber, 2013
Architektur Architecture SOM – Skidmore,
Owings & Merrill
Projekt Project John Jay College of Criminal
Justice, New York (US), 2011

Bühne: Nutzungskontext

Foto **Photo** Zita Oberwalder, aus **from** don't talk to the sailor moon, Pok Fu Lam Road, Hongkong (RC), 2011

Foto Photo Rupert Steiner, 2008
Architektur Architecture Architekten Tillner & Willinger
Projekt Project Bürohaus Office building Skyline Spittelau,
Wien (AT), 2008

Bühne: Nutzungskontext

Foto **Photo** Hertha Hurnaus, Fotoessay **photo-essay**
in: Weltkulturerbe in Österreich, Band I, **World**
Heritage in Austria, Vol. 1 voraussichtlich **expected** in 2016
Architektur **Architecture** Carl von Ghega
Projekt **Project** Krauselklauseviadukt, Semmering-
bahn, Breitenstein (AT), 1854

Foto **Photo** Stefan Oláh, 13., Kennedybrücke,
Wien (AT), aus **from** Fünfundneunzig Wiener
Würstelstände – The Hot 95, 2011

Foto Photo Margherita Spiluttini, 2003
Architektur Architecture Herzog & de Meuron
Projekt Project Zwei gläserne Flügelbauten am
Girtannersberg, Helvetia Versicherungen Helvetia
insurance, St. Gallen (CH), 2002

144

Bühne: Nutzungskontext

Foto Photo Margherita Spiluttini, aus der Serie
from the series Nach der Natur Beyond Nature, 2000
Architektur Architecture Christian Menn
Projekt Project Via Mala Autobahnbrücke
Highway bridge, Via Mala (CH), 1965

Foto Photo Markus Bstieler, 2010
Architektur Architecture Massimiliano Fuksas
Projekt Project Palestra di Paliano,
Paliano (IT), 1985

Foto Photo Günter Richard Wett, 2012
Architektur Architecture ao-architekten
Projekt Project Kapelle Chapel Schaufeljoch,
Neustift im Stubaital (AT), 2012

Bühne: Nutzungskontext

Foto **Photo** Paul Ott, 2004
Architektur **Architecture** SPLITTERWERK
Projekt **Project** Green Treefrog,
St. Josef (AT), 2004

147

Bühne: Nutzungskontext

Foto Photo Pez Hejduk, 2009
Architektur Architecture unbekannt unknown
Projekt Project Steigerturm der Rettungs- und
Feuerwehrleitstelle, Feldkirch (AT)

Foto Photo Angelo Kaunat, 1997
Architektur Architecture Kiessler + Partner
Projekt Project Literaturhaus München,
München (DE), 1997

149

Foto Photo Lukas Schaller, 2009

Architektur Architecture Mario Fiorentino

Projekt Project Nuovo Corviale, südlich von Rom

south of Rome (IT), 1982

Foto Photo Dietmar Tollerian/Archipicture, 2006
Architektur Architecture Ursula Nikodem-Edlinger,
Danijele Tolanov, BASEhabitat, Kunstuniversität Linz
Projekt Project Baya Kindergarten, Orange Farm,
Johannesburg (ZA), 2006

Foto **Photo** Pia Odorizzi, 2007
Architektur **Architecture** peterlorenzateliers
Projekt **Project** Q19, Einkaufszentrum **Shopping mall**,
Wien (AT), 2005

Bühne: Nutzungskontext

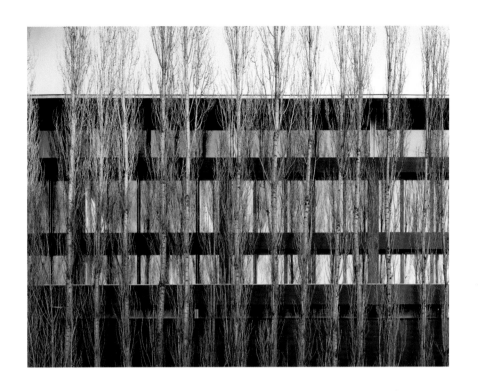

Foto Photo Angelo Kaunat, 1998
Architektur Architecture DFZ Architekten
Projekt Project HEW Verwaltung,
Hamburg (DE), 1999

Foto Photo Angelo Kaunat, 2008
Architektur Architecture Ben van Berkel – UNStudio
Projekt Project MUMUTH – Haus für Musik und
Musiktheater House of music and musical theatre,
Graz (AT), 2008

Foto Photo Markus Kaiser, 2014
Architektur Architecture Shigeru Ban Architects
Projekt Project GC Osaka Building,
Osaka (JP), 2000

Foto Photo Bruno Klomfar, 2012
Architektur Architecture Gerhard Steixner
Projekt Project Presshaus Winepress building Jöchl,
Langenzersdorf (AT), 2012

155

Foto Photo Alexander Eugen Koller, Brigittenau,
Wien (AT), 2014

Foto Photo Alexander Eugen Koller, Alsergrund,
Wien (AT), 2014

Bühne: Nutzungskontext

Foto Photo Alexander Eugen Koller, Allgemeines
Krankenhaus General hospital, Wien (AT), 2014

Foto Photo Markus Kaiser, 2015
Architektur Architecture querkraft architekten,
Scheifinger + Partner, F + P Architekten
Projekt Project City Gate, Wien (AT), 2015

158

Foto **Photo** Gisela Erlacher, Jiulongzhen,
Chongqing (RC), 2011

Foto **Photo** Peter Eder, 1996
Architektur **Architecture** Pierre Jeanneret,
B.P. Mathur
Projekt **Project** Fine Arts Museum,
Chandigarh (IN), 1968

Foto Photo Gisela Erlacher, 2011
Architektur Architecture gmp – Architekten
von Gerkan, Marg und Partner
Projekt Project Grand Theatre,
Chongqing (RC), 2009

160

Bühne: Nutzungskontext

Foto Photo Hertha Hurnaus, Fotoessay photo-essay
aus from Harry Glück. Wohnbauten,
Hg. ed. Reinhard Seiß, Müry Salzmann Verlag, 2013
Architektur Architecture Harry Glück,
Kurt Hlaweniczka, Requat & Reinthaller & Partner
Architekten
Projekt Project Wohnpark Residential park Alt Erlaa,
Wien (AT), 1985

Handschrift
Signature

: Vom Nutzen der Wiedererkennbarkeit
: On the Uses of Recognizability

Obwohl er nicht die Illusion habe, „Fotografie könne die eigentliche Wirkung von Architektur und ihren Innenräumen wirklich vermitteln", beauftragt der Architekt Rainer Köberl immer denselben Fotografen, um parallel zu seinen Bauten „ein homogenes ‚Bildwerk' entstehen zu lassen". In der Architekturgeschichte gibt es Werkserien, die untrennbar mit der Handschrift einzelner Fotografinnen und Fotografen verbunden sind. Architektur und Fotografie verstärken wechselseitig ihre Signifikanz. Geht das so weit, dass mögliche Bilder bereits den architektonischen Entwurfsvorgang prägen oder dass umgekehrt architektonische Konzepte die fotografische Arbeit verändern?

Die Architekturvermittlerinnen und -vermittler, die wir für diese Publikation befragt haben, sind sich einig, dass Architekturfotografie weit über das Dokumentarische hinausgeht. Ihre Kommentare beschreiben, wie Fotografie das „Wesen der dargestellten Architektur" (Theresia Hauenfels) erfasst und was passiert, wenn Menschen „nicht nur maßstabgebendes Beiwerk sind, sondern zu den Helden einer Kurzgeschichte werden" (Oliver Elser). Sie schätzen, dass es eben nicht darum geht, „ein spektakuläres Bauwerk ins Bild zu setzen", sondern darum, zu fokussieren, was „für die Situation charakteristisch und wesentlich erscheint" (Sebastian Hackenschmidt). Es gefällt ihnen, wenn Ausschnitt und Licht so eingesetzt werden, dass eine Skulptur aus Stein „suggestiv zum Leben erweckt wird" (Otto Kapfinger). Der Schriftsteller Franz Schuh erkennt in der fotografischen Handschrift eine literarische Technik wieder, „das Zitat. Zitieren ist eine Kunst, nicht bloß die Wiedergabe von etwas Vorgegebenem." Bei alldem ist die spezifische Handschrift, so Judith Eiblmayr, „weniger rein technischer Natur; sondern vielmehr die spezifische Sichtweise, die persönlich motivierte ‚Rahmung' des Objekts". AF

Although he harbors no illusion that "photography can genuinely convey the impact of architecture and its interior spaces", the architect Rainer Köberl always commissions the same photographer, thereby allowing "a homogenous 'image inventory' to emerge" in conjunction with his buildings. In architectural history, there are series of buildings that are inseparable from the signature of a certain photographer. Architecture and photography enhance one another's significance reciprocally. Does this extend so far that potential images already shape architectural design processes or, conversely, that architectural concepts modify photographic approaches?

The architectural intermediaries we interviewed for this publication are in agreement that architectural photography goes far beyond the documentary. Their commentary characterizes the way in which photography grasps the "essence of the depicted architecture" (Theresia Hauenfels) and what happens when people "are more than props that provide a sense of scale, and instead become the heroes of a short story" (Oliver Elser). They are well aware that it is not a question of "providing an image of a spectacular building" but instead of focusing on that which "appears characteristic of and essential to a situation" (Sebastian Hackenschmidt). They derive enjoyment from the way in which framing and lighting are deployed so that a sculpture in stone "is awakened to life in suggestive ways" (Otto Kapfinger). In photographic signature, the writer Franz Schuh recognizes a literary technique, namely "the quotation. Citation is an art, not the mere recapitulation of something pre-existent." Judith Eiblmayr claims that a specific manner is "less purely technical in nature than a certain way of seeing, a personally motivated 'framing' of the object." AF

Foto Photo Hertha Hurnaus, 2006
Architektur Architecture Rafael Moneo
Projekt Project Palacio de Congresos y
Auditorio, San Sebastián (ES), 1999

Foto Photo Hertha Hurnaus, 2006
Architektur Architecture
the next ENTERprise – architects
Projekt Project Seebad Lakeside bath Caldaro,
Kaltern (IT), 2006

164

„Sind es sorgsame Inszenierungen oder hat Hertha Hurnaus immer wieder den moment décisif erwischt, jenen entscheidenden Moment, den der Fotograf Henri Cartier-Bresson als das Ziel seiner Arbeit beschrieben hat? Es gibt im Werk von Hertha Hurnaus unzählige Bilder, die so unwahrscheinlich sind, dass sie wohl mit arrangierten Schauspielern entstanden sein müssen. Aber das, schwört die Fotografin, ist eher selten der Fall.

Doch worin besteht der alles entscheidende Moment in der Architekturfotografie? Darin, dass die Menschen auf den Bildern in dieser Sekunde nicht nur maßstabgebendes Beiwerk sind, sondern zu den Helden einer Kurzgeschichte werden, die Hertha Hurnaus in unseren Köpfen anzustoßen vermag."

Oliver Elser, Kurator am Deutschen Architekturmuseum, Frankfurt am Main

"Is all of this just meticulous staging, or has Hertha Hurnaus always managed to seize the moment décisif that Henri Cartier-Bresson characterized as the aim of his labors? In Hertha Hurnaus's œuvre, one encounters countless images that seem so improbable one is tempted to assume they were created with the assistance of actors. But this, she assures us, has seldom been the case.

What accounts for the decisive moment in an architectural photograph? That, in this instant, the people visible in the image are more than props providing a sense of scale but instead become the heroes of a short story, one that Hertha Hurnaus is able to set in motion in our minds."

Oliver Elser, curator, Deutsches Architekturmuseum, Frankfurt am Main

Foto Photo Hertha Hurnaus, Fotoessay photo-essay aus from Harry Glück. Wohnbauten, Hg. ed. Reinhard Seiß, Müry Salzmann Verlag, 2013
Architektur Architecture Harry Glück, Kurt Hlaweniczka, Requat & Reinthaller & Partner Architekten
Projekt Project Wohnpark Residential park Alt Erlaa, Wien (AT), 1985

Foto Photo Markus Bstieler, 2013
Architektur Architecture Peter Zumthor
Projekt Project Werkraum Bregenzerwald,
Andelsbuch (AT), 2013

Foto Photo Markus Bstieler, 2007
Architektur Architecture Zaha Hadid Architects
Projekt Project Hungerburgbahn Innsbruck,
Innsbruck (AT), 2007

Foto Photo Markus Bstieler, 2013
Architektur Architecture Peter Zumthor
Projekt Project Werkraum Bregenzerwald,
Andelsbuch (AT), 2013

Foto Photo Gisela Erlacher, aus from cut,
Klagenfurt (AT), 2010

„Künstlerisch haben diese Bilder Eigenart ohne Gepränge, paradoxerweise, indem sie vergebliche Bemühungen zeigen, eine Umwelt eigenartig mit ‚Stil' zu gestalten. Man sieht, wie diese Versuche, einer Umwelt etwas Unverwechselbares, etwas geradezu Künstlerisches, etwas Schönes hinzuzufügen, scheitern – und das ist eine weitere Kunst dieser Fotografien: Es sind viele Bilder, die man am Ende auch als ein Bild gesehen haben kann. [...]

Man sieht, Geschmack ist gerade das, worüber man streiten kann. Aber die Fotografin streitet nicht mithilfe von Satire oder Polemik. Sie verwendet in ihrer Auseinandersetzung ein Verfahren, das vor allem aus der Literatur bekannt ist: das Zitat. Zitieren ist eine Kunst, also nicht bloß die Wiedergabe von etwas Vorgegebenem. Erlachers Art des Zitierens, die von ihr gewählten Ausschnitte der architektonischen Misere, machen diese erst deutlich. Eine Ästhetik des Hässlichen tut sich auf und lehrt den Betrachter, über das zu staunen, was er selber schon oft genug gesehen hat."

Franz Schuh, Schriftsteller

"In artistic terms, these images possess their uniqueness, but without ostentation paradoxically because they display the futile effort to shape an environment idiosyncratically by means of 'style'. One observes the necessary failure of these attempts to add something unmistakable, something essentially artistic, something beautiful, to an environment – and that is the larger art of these photographs. That is, in the end, many of these pictures are perceptible as one image. [...]

Clearly, taste is subject to dispute. But the photographer does not argue by means of satire or polemics. In her examinations, she exploits a procedure that is known primarily from literature, namely, the quotation. Citation is an art, not the mere recapitulation of something pre-existent. Erlacher's approach to citation, the details of architectural misery she selects, makes this clear. She takes advantage of an esthetic of ugliness, teaching viewers to be astonished at what they have seen often enough previously."

Franz Schuh, writer

Foto Photo Gisela Erlacher, Details (Details),
Klein-Neusiedl (AT), 2005

169

Foto Photo Eduard Hueber, 1993

Architektur Architecture Simon Ungers mit with
Tom Kinslow
Projekt Project T-House, Wilton,
New York (US), 1992

Foto **Photo** Eduard Hueber, Ithaca Sky,
Landschaft nahe **Landscape near** Ithaca,
Upstate New York (US), 2000

Foto Photo Günter Richard Wett, 2006
Architektur Architecture Kenzo Tange
Projekt Project Tokyo Metropolitan Government
Building, Tokio (JP), 1991

Foto Photo Günter Richard Wett, 2010
Architektur Architecture Herzog & de Meuron
Projekt Project VitraHaus, Weil am Rhein (DE), 2010

Foto Photo Günter Richard Wett, 2004
Architektur Architecture Rainer Köberl,
Giner + Wucherer
Projekt Project Sudhaus Brewery Adambräu,
Innsbruck (AT), 2004

173

Foto Photo Margherita Spiluttini, 1987

Architektur Architecture Johann Ferdinand
Hetzendorf von Hohenberg

Projekt Project Römische Ruine im Schönbrunner
Schlosspark Roman ruin in the park of Schönbrunn
palace, Wien (AT), 1778

Linke Seite: „Dies war von Anfang an eines meiner Lieblingsbilder, weil es so fotografiert ist, Ausschnitt, Licht so gewählt wurden, dass sich die Skulptur aus Stein im Gravitationszentrum aller Richtungsvektoren der Bildkomposition befindet und dadurch so gesetzt ist, dass sie suggestiv zum Leben erweckt wird. Es ist also die Umkehrung der künstlichen Ruine, die Gegenbewegung zum Verfall des Steins in die Natur – in der Skulptur fast die Fleischwerdung des Steins."

Otto Kapfinger, Architekturpublizist

Left page: "This was my favorite picture from the beginning because it is photographed in such a way – the selection of cropping and lighting – that the stone sculpture is located at the gravitational center of all of the composition's vectors, positioned so suggestively that it comes to life. It therefore reverses the artistic ruin, moves in a direction contrary to the deterioration of stone in nature – in the sculpture, we almost witness an incarnation, a becoming-flesh, of the stone."

Otto Kapfinger, architectural journalist

Foto Photo Margherita Spiluttini, 1989
Architektur Architecture Paul Engelmann,
Ludwig Wittgenstein
Projekt Project Haus Wittgenstein, Wittgenstein
house, Wien (AT), 1928

Foto **Photo** Alexander Eugen Koller, 2009
Architektur **Architecture** Benda & Walles
Projekt **Project** Apothekengebäude und Einfami-
lienhaus **Apothecary building and single family house,**
Leopoldsdorf im Marchfelde (AT), 2010

Foto **Photo** Alexander Eugen Koller, 2014
Architektur **Architecture** Benda & Walles
Projekt **Project** Einfamilienhaus **Single family house**
Hugo-Kirsch-Gasse, Wien (AT), 2014

Foto Photo Manfred Seidl, 2012

Architektur Architecture Werner Neuwirth

Projekt Project Wohnbebauung Housing estate

Donaufelder Straße, BPL 1+2, Wien (AT), 2012

Foto Photo Manfred Seidl, 2012
Architektur Architecture Werner Neuwirth
Projekt Project Wohnbebauung Housing estate
Donaufelder Straße, BPL 1+2, Wien (ΛT), 2012

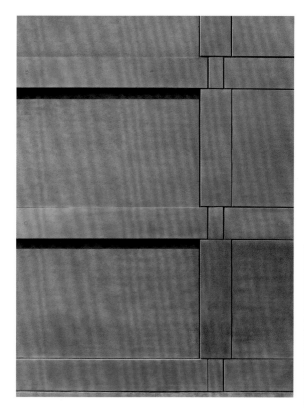

Foto Photo Manfred Seidl, 2012
Architektur Architecture Werner Neuwirth
Projekt Project Wohnbebauung Housing estate
Donaufelder Straße, BPL 1+2, Wien (AT), 2012

Foto Photo Pez Hejduk, 2013
Architektur Architecture Karl Alois Krist
Projekt Project Wohnhausanlage Social housing estate
Gemeindebau Liebknechthof, Wien (AT), 1927

Foto Photo Pez Hejduk, 2001
Architektur Architecture Joseph Maria Olbrich
Projekt Project Wiener Secession, Wien (AT), 1898
Ausstellungsansicht Exhibition view Roman Ondák,
SK parking, 2001

„Das Objektivist nur vermeintlich objektiv; zu subjektiv ist das hinter dem optischen Gerät operierende Subjekt – es ist die Fotografin, die die Eindrücklichkeit eines abzubildenden Objekts bestimmt. Die spezifische Handschrift ist wohl weniger rein technischer Natur als vielmehr die spezifische Sichtweise, die persönlich motivierte ‚Rahmung' des Objekts."

Judith Eiblmayr, Architektin, Architekturkritikerin

"It can be argued that the objectivist is only putatively objective; the individual who operates the optical apparatus is invariably subjective – it is the photographer who determines the impression made by the depicted object. Arguably, a particular signature is less technical in nature and more a specific way of seeing, the personally motivated 'framing' of the object."

Judith Eiblmayr, architect and architectural critic

Foto Photo Pez Hejduk, 1998
Architektur Architecture Joseph Maria Olbrich
Projekt Project Die rote Secession – Projekt von
Marcus Geiger anlässlich des 100-jährigen
Jubiläums der Wiener Secession The red secession –
project by Marcus Geiger celebrating the centennial of the
Vienna Secession, Wien (AT), 1998

Foto Photo Dietmar Tollerian /Archipicture, aus from
Unscharfe Grenzen (Blurred boundaries) – Annäherungen
zwischen Kunst und Bau, Beispiel: Oberösterreich
(Convergences between art and building, for instance:
Upper Austria), hg. von ed. by afo, Linz, 2011
Architektur Architecture Riepl Riepl Architekten
Projekt Project OK – Offenes Kulturhaus Oberöster-
reich, Linz (AT), 1998

Handschrift: Vom Nutzen der Wiedererkennbarkeit

Foto **Photo** Dietmar Tollerian / Archipicture, 2012
Architektur **Architecture** Dominique Perrault architecture
Projekt **Project** Vienna DC Towers, Wien (AT), 2014

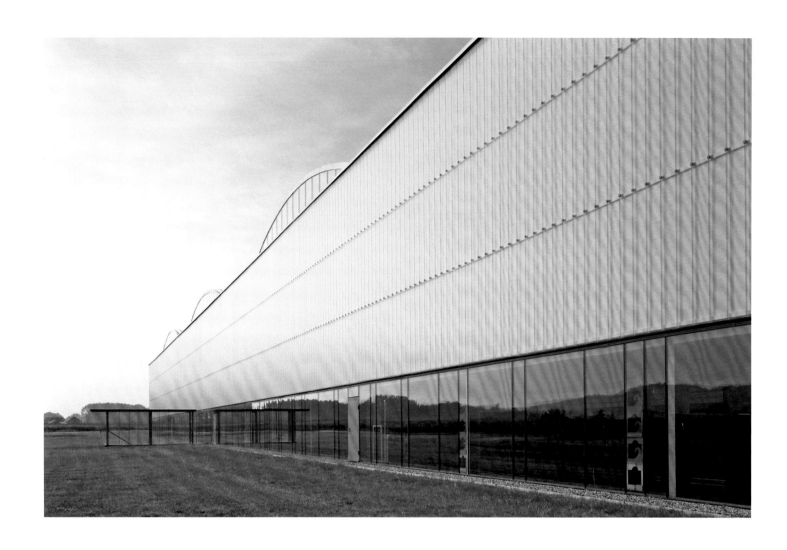

Foto **Photo** Pia Odorizzi, 2003
Architektur **Architecture** Andreas Ortner
Projekt **Project** Peneder, St. Martin (AT), 2003

Foto Photo Markus Kaiser, 2015
Architektur Architecture Zaha Hadid Architects
Projekt Project Riverside Museum,
Glasgow (GB), 2011

Foto Photo Markus Kaiser, 2014
Architektur Architecture Tadao Ando
Projekt Project Church of the Light, Ibaraki,
Osaka (JP), 1989

Foto **Photo** Zita Oberwalder, 2012

Architektur **Architecture** Gerhard Mitterberger

Projekt **Project** Haus der Generationen

House of generations Eggersdorf,

Eggersdorf bei Graz (AT), 2011

„Ihre fotografische Herangehensweise ist mit ‚klassisch' insofern unzureichend definiert, als man den Begriff des ‚Modernismus', mit dem der Transfer des Repertoires der Moderne in die nächsten Generationen bezeichnet wird, zwar in der bildenden Kunst kennt, jedoch keine Entsprechung in der Fotografie existiert. ‚Klassisch' heißt bei Oberwalder keineswegs statisch, sondern meint ein Wiederaufgreifen eines fotografischen Vokabulars, das Fokus, Perspektive, Komposition oder Tonalität aus der Kamera heraus anlegt. Dass für Oberwalder dabei die Architektur und die Architekturfotografie eine große Rolle spielen, bestätigt, dass auch die Fotografie ein unvollendetes Projekt der Moderne ist, das stets befragt und wieder aufgegriffen werden kann."

outstanding artist award – künstlerische Fotografie 2014, Bundeskanzleramt Österreich,

Text: Dr. Susanne Neuburger (Jurybegründung, Auszug), Jury: Christine Frisinghelli, Aglaia Konrad,

Dr. Susanne Neuburger

"Her approach to photography is inadequately defined with the term 'classical', since the term 'modernism' refers to the transfer of a modernist repertoire to subsequent generations, a process familiar in the fine arts, which, however, has no counterpart in photography. With Oberwalder, 'classical' hardly means static but instead the renewal of a photographic vocabulary, one that allows focus, perspective, composition, and tonality to be structured by the camera. That architecture and architectural photography play a major role for Oberwalder confirms the fact that photography, too, is an unfinished project of modernity and one that can be continually interrogated and revisited."

outstanding artist award – artistic photography, 2014, Federal Chancellery,

Austria, text: Dr. Susanne Neuburger, (jury decision, excerpt),

jury: Christine Frisinghelli, Aglaia Konrad, Dr. Susanne Neuburger

Foto **Photo** Zita Oberwalder, 2014
Architektur **Architecture** Gerhard Mitterberger
Projekt **Project** Schauraum Autohaus **Automobile showroom** Prisker, Lienz (AT), 2014

Foto Photo Angelo Kaunat, 2001
Architektur Architecture Herzog & de Meuron
Projekt Project Fünf Höfe, München (DE),
erste Phase first phase 2001

Foto Photo Angelo Kaunat, 2001
Architektur Architecture Massimiliano Fuksas
Projekt Project Vienna Twin Towers,
Wien (AT), 2001

Foto Photo Angelo Kaunat, 2005
Architektur Architecture Adolph-Herbert Kelz
Projekt Project Haus House Krispl, Graz (AT), 2005

Foto Photo Bruno Klomfar, 2010
Architektur Architecture Marte.Marte Architekten
Projekt Project Volksschule Primary school Wels-Mauth,
Wels (AT), 2009

Foto Photo Bruno Klomfar, 2012
Architektur Architecture Marte.Marte Architekten
Projekt Project Schutzhütte Mountain hut,
Laterns (AT), 2011

„Über das rein Dokumentarische hinausgehend, befasst sich Bruno Klomfar mit der Komposition von Raumstrukturen. In seiner klaren Bildsprache treten geometrische Zusammenhänge deutlich zutage. Dabei lässt er die Betrachterinnen und Betrachter am räumlichen Erleben der von ihm porträtierten Bauten und Orte teilhaben. Materialität und Lichtstimmung akzentuieren die präzisen Bilder, die bei jedem Sujet aufs Neue das Wesen der dargestellten Architektur mit konzentriertem Blick ergründen."

Theresia Hauenfels, Autorin und Kuratorin

"Going beyond purely documentary aspects, Bruno Klomfar is preoccupied with the composition of spatial structures. In his lucid pictorial idiom, geometrical relationships are distinctly brought out. At the same time, viewers are invited to experience the spatiality of the buildings and locations he portrays. Materiality and light effects accentuate his meticulous images, whose concentrated gaze penetrates the essence of the depicted architecture in new ways."

Theresia Hauenfels, author and curator

Foto **Photo** Bruno Klomfar, 2003
Architektur **Architecture** Steinmayr Mascher
Projekt **Project** Filmmuseum, Wien (AT), 2003

„Mit nüchternem Blick und mit sorgfältiger Aufmerksamkeit für Atmosphäre, Details und den richtigen Moment erfasst Stefan Oláh die Eigenart von Architektur, ohne ihre Umgebung und ihren Kontext aus dem Auge zu verlieren. Als Fotograf zeigt er architektonische Sachverhalte ohne Effekthascherei oder technische Spielereien. Bei der Aufnahme der futuristisch-technoiden Tankstelle zwischen Burgtheater und Volksgarten geht es folglich nicht darum, ein spektakuläres Bauwerk ins Bild zu setzen; vielmehr fokussiert er auf das, was ihm für die Situation charakteristisch und wesentlich erscheint. So hat er keineswegs auszublenden versucht, dass das Areal um das Burgtheater als Parkplatz genutzt wird. Die Tankstelle wurde ja auch nicht für die Fiaker an diesem prominenten Ort aufgestellt.“

Sebastian Hackenschmidt, Kustos und Kurator am MAK, Wien

Foto **Photo** Stephan Oláh, AWI Diskont,
Josef Meinrad Platz, Wien (AT), aus **from**
Sechsundzwanzig Wiener Tankstellen, Wien, 2009

"With a sober gaze and with painstaking attentiveness to atmosphere, details, and the right moment, Stefan Oláh captures the uniqueness of architecture without losing sight of the surroundings and the context. As a photographer, he displays architectural reality without resorting to empty showmanship or technical gimmickry. Hence, with his images of the futuristic-technoid gas station between the Burgtheater and the Volksgarten, it is not a question of creating a mise en scène for a spectacular edifice; instead, his focus is on what strikes him as characteristic and essential about the situation. He has by no means attempted to disguise the fact that the premises around the Burgtheater are used for parking. Nor was the gas station set up at this prominent location for the horse-drawn carriage."

Sebastian Hackenschmidt, curator at the MAK, Vienna

„Der Fotograf Rupert Steiner arbeitet präzise im baulichen Sachverhalt. Er braucht keine Anleitung zu Besonderheit, Ablichtungsstandort oder Bildausschnitt eines Bauwerks. Er arbeitet am liebsten allein mit dem Objekt und lässt es auf sich wirken. Dabei erkundet er, was ein Bauwerk ausmacht – dessen materielle und immaterielle Aura. Schließlich hält er das Vorgefundene mit wenigen, aber umso aussagekräftigeren Bildern fest. Nicht mehr, aber auch nicht weniger."

Walter Stelzhammer, Architekt

"The photographer Rupert Steiner approaches his architectural subjects with precision. He requires no introduction to a building's peculiarities, location, or field of vision. He prefers working alone with the object, letting it affect him however it will. He explores that which constitutes a given structure – its material and immaterial aura. Finally, he captures his motifs through a small number of images that are all the more powerfully expressive. No more, but also no less."

Walter Stelzhammer, architect

Foto Photo Rupert Steiner, 1997
Architektur Architecture Walter Stelzhammer
Projekt Project Maison Turquoise,
Ölüdeniz (TR), 2000

193

Foto Photo Paul Ott, 2008
Architektur Architecture SPLITTERWERK
Projekt Project Frog Queen, Graz (AT), 2007

Foto **Photo** Peter Eder, 1999
Architektur **Architecture** Bearth & Deplazes
Projekt **Project** Schule mit Halle **School with hall,**
Vella (CH), 1998

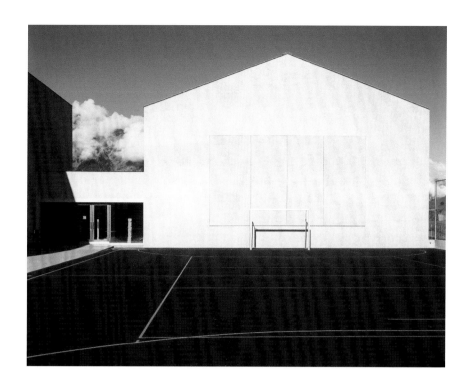

Foto **Photo** Peter Eder, 2013
Architektur **Architecture** Zach (1952),
Bramberger architects (2012)
Projekt **Project** Künstlerhaus, Graz (AT)

„Schaller ist ein eindeutiger Verfechter des Einzelbildes. Im sicheren Wissen, dass einhundert Fabrikansichten ohnehin nicht die Wirklichkeit einer Fabrik preisgäben, setzt er auf die suggestive Wirkung des einzelnen Tableaus. Seine wohl organisierten Bilder sind keine bloßen Bestandsaufnahmen architektonischer Objekte. In subjektiv gewählten Blickwinkeln charakterisiert er die dargestellten Gebäude und nimmt dabei die Vernachlässigung von Schauseiten und baulichen Details durchaus in Kauf."

Fabian Knierim, Kurator WestLicht. Schauplatz für Fotografie

"Schaller is a decisive proponent of the individual image. Secure in the knowledge that one hundred views of a factory by no means disclose its reality, he relies upon the suggestive effects of the individual tableau. His well-composed pictures are more than mere inventories of architecture objects. With subjectively shaped viewing angles, he characterizes the depicted buildings, fully aware of the sacrifice involved in disregarding principal fronts and structural details."

Fabian Knierim, curator, WestLicht. Schauplatz für Fotografie

Foto **Photo** Lukas Schaller, No Ball Games,
London (GB), 2004

196

Foto **Photo** Lukas Schaller, Agip Gas Stazione,
Tivoli (IT), 2009

Künstlichkeit
Artificiality

: Vom Nutzen der Inszenierung
: On the Uses of Staging

Die Produktion und die Betrachtung von Fotografien können nicht losgelöst von historischen Konventionen verstanden werden. Le Corbusier setzte vor seinen Villen Automobile in Szene, um den Aufbruch in die Moderne zu signalisieren, während der Fotograf Julius Shulman das scheinbar zwanglose Leben des kalifornischen Traums inszenierte. Neben dem kulturellen Kontext geht es auch um anthropologische Konstanten, die von der Architekturfotografie bestätigt oder ins Wanken gebracht werden. Welchen Beobachterstandpunkt nehmen Fotos ein? Folgen sie dem menschlichen Auge und seinen Wahrnehmungsgewohnheiten oder erfinden sie ihre eigenen physikalischen Gesetzmäßigkeiten? Perspektiven kollidieren, Maßstäbe täuschen, Kameras scheinen in der Luft zu schweben. Ein Spiegelkabinett baut sich auf, das die Bewohnerinnen und Bewohner hoffentlich nicht jeden Tag so schwindelerregend erleben.

Mit Mitteln der Inszenierung kann ein Foto das epistemische Feld eines Objekts verstärken, also das, was uns ein Gegenstand erzählen, was er ans Licht bringen will. Das Modell einer Polarstation wird in geheimnisvoll kühles Licht getaucht. Schon wenige Gegenstände und deren gezielte Positionierung im Raum verleiten zu Spekulationen über den Lebensstil der Menschen. Die Fotografinnen und Fotografen benutzen die Architektur, um kleine Dramen zu inszenieren. Im 21. Jahrhundert muss die Konkurrenz durch computergenerierte Bilder zwangsläufig mitgedacht werden: die Ästhetik der Renderings, die immer detailgetreuer werden, schöner als die Wirklichkeit, lebendiger als das Leben. Auch in der Fotografie lassen sich Modell und gebaute Realität mitunter nur schwer unterscheiden, zumindest im Hinblick auf ihre Präsenz und Aussagekraft. Und manchmal wirkt bereits die Architektur selbst so künstlich, als stamme sie aus der digitalen Trickkiste. AF

The production and contemplation of photographs cannot be understood without considering historical conventions. To signal the inception of modernity, Le Corbusier displayed automobiles in front of his villas, while the photographer Julius Shulman stage-managed the seemingly unconstrained life of the California dream. Alongside the cultural context, certain anthropological constants are either confirmed or undermined by architectural photography. Which observer's position is adopted in a given photograph? Is it faithful to the human eye and its perceptual habits or does it devise its own physical principles? Perspectives collide, relationships of scale deceive, cameras seem to hover in the air. A house of mirrors assembles itself, one that hopefully the residents do not experience so vertiginously every day.

By using the resources of mise en scène, a photograph can strengthen the object's epistemic field, that is to say, that which the object tells us, that which it strives to bring to light. The model of a polar station is bathed in a cool, enigmatic light. Just a few objects and their purposeful placement in space prompt speculations concerning the lifestyle of the inhabitants. Photographers exploit architecture in order to stage mini-dramas. In the 21st century, it becomes indispensable to consider the competition represented by the computer-generated image, the aesthetic of renderings, ever more detailed, more exquisite than reality, more lively than life itself. Even in photography, the model and the reality are often difficult to distinguish from one another, at least with regard to their presence and expressive force. At times, moreover, the architecture itself seems so artificial that it could almost be the product of the digital bag of tricks. AF

Foto Photo Angelo Kaunat, 1996
Architektur Architecture Ateliers Jean Nouvel
Projekt Project Galeries Lafayette Berlin,
Berlin (DE), 1996

Künstlichkeit: Vom Nutzen der Inszenierung

Foto Photo Alexander Eugen Koller, 2001
Architektur Architecture Ateliers Jean Nouvel
Projekt Project Gasometer Simmering, Bauteil A
Building component A , Wien (AT), 2001

Foto **Photo** Eduard Hueber, 2013
Architektur **Architecture** Baumschlager Eberle
Projekt **Project** 2226, Lustenau (AT), 2013

Künstlichkeit: Vom Nutzen der Inszenierung

Foto Photo Manfred Seidl, 2014
Architektur Architecture S/S/S Soyka Silber Soyka
Architekten
Projekt Project Siemens City, Wien (AT), 2010

Foto Photo Angelo Kaunat, 2008
Architektur Architecture LP architektur
Projekt Project Haus House Peneder,
Atzbach (AT), 2008

Foto **Photo** Alexander Eugen Koller, Ohne Titel
untitled, Tauern Autobahn (AT), 2014

Foto Photo Pia Odorizzi, 1989

Architektur Architecture Karl Odorizzi

Projekt Project Wohnhaus House – Im Windschatten
leben (Living on the lee side), Gmunden (AT), 1975

Foto Photo Manfred Seidl, 2004
Architektur Architecture MAGNA Liegenschafts-
verwaltung
Projekt Project Clubhaus Golfclub Club house
golf club FONTANA, Oberwaltersdorf (AT), 2004

Foto Photo Peter Eder, 2009
Architektur Architecture weichlbauer/ortis
Projekt Project Bauernhaus Farmhouse
surplus value_01, Laufnitzdorf (AT), 2009

Foto Photo Lukas Schaller, 2005
Architektur Architecture Duncan Lewis, Hervé Potin,
BLOCK Architectes
Projekt Project Cité Manifeste,
Muhlhouse (FR), 2005

Foto Photo Paul Ott, Freiwillige Feuerwehr
Volunteer fire department,
Bairisch-Kölldorf (AT), 2008

208

Foto **Photo** Rupert Steiner, 2000
Architektur **Architecture** the unit
Projekt **Project** Jet2Web, Flagshipstore,
Wien (AT), 2000

Foto Photo Hertha Hurnaus, 2013
Architektur Architecture Veech x Veech
Projekt Project ORF 1 News Studio,
Wien (AT), 2013

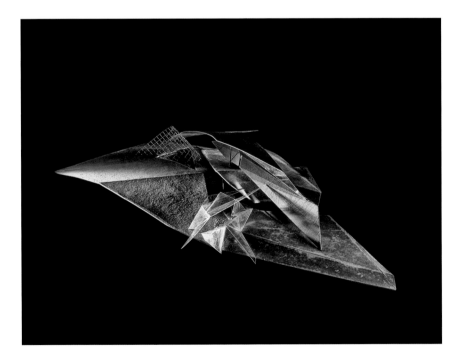

Foto Photo Alexander Eugen Koller, 2004
Architektur Architecture Lola Rieger
Projekt Project Modell Model Polarstation

Foto Photo Lukas Schaller, 2006
Architektur Architecture
the next ENTERprise – architects
Projekt Project Modell Model Wolkenturm
Grafenegg

Foto Photo Lukas Schaller, 2007
Architektur Architecture
the next ENTERprise – architects
Projekt Project Wolkenturm Grafenegg,
Grafenegg (AT), 2007

Foto Photo Paul Ott, 2009

Temporäre Architektur Temporary architecture

Peter Kaschnig

Projekt Project hausblau, Klagenfurt (AT), 2009

Foto Photo Zita Oberwalder, 2012

Künstler Artist E.d Gfrerer

Projekt Project Floßwärter-Häuschen Shelter for raft
attendant, Modell Model 1:2, Graz (AT), 2012

Foto Photo Zita Oberwalder, 2014
Künstler Artist Mirko Maric
Projekt Project Pazi zivot (Achtung Leben
Attention life), Velika Avlija (Großer Garten
Large garden), Sarajevo (BIH), 2014

Foto **Photo** Hertha Hurnaus, aus **from** Ausstellung
exhibition Baukultur – Denk deine Stadt anders!
(**Building culture – think your city differently!**),
Zusammenarbeit mit **collaboration with** feld72,
inspirin, nonconform, Wien (AT), 2014

Foto **Photo** Rupert Steiner, 2007
Architektur **Architecture** Casa Pendente, Parco dei
Mostri, Bomarzo (IT), 1585

Foto Photo Zita Oberwalder, aus from don't talk
to the sailor moon, Hongkong (RC), 2011

Foto **Photo** Gisela Erlacher, Shenzhen
Jiefangbei (RC), 2012

Wiederverwertung
Reuse

: Umnutzung
: Conversion

In Architektur und Städtebau ist die Umnutzung längst zu einer wichtigen Aufgabe geworden. Die Wiederverwertung bestehender Strukturen entspricht dem Gebot der Nachhaltigkeit, und die Wiederbelebung historischer Gebäude stiftet Identität. Manche Bilder dokumentieren tiefgreifende Umbauten, wie etwa die Transformation einer Bierbrauerei zur Ausstellungshalle, die Umwandlung eines gründerzeitlichen Ladenlokals in eine Tankstelle, eines herrschaftlichen Palais zum bürgerlichen Museum. Ein luftiger Expo-Pavillon benötigt einige bautechnische Ertüchtigung, um museumstauglich zu werden, während ein betonierter Uferstreifen mit wenigen Eingriffen zur Strandbar wird. Andere Bilder werden Zeugen von temporären Umnutzungen, bei denen ein Ausstellungspavillon zum Berg mutiert, eine Tunnelröhre zum Festzelt, eine Autobahnbrücke zum Wohnzimmer, ein leer stehendes Erdgeschoss zum Hotelzimmer. Manche Orte warten noch auf ihre Umnutzung: Vor einer alten Markhalle wurden bereits die Baucontainer in Stellung gebracht. Oder betreffen sie das Nachbarsgrundstück? Es kommt auch vor, dass Architekturbüros ihre eigenen Ikonen umbauen: In New York konvertieren SOM ein Bankgebäude aus den 1950er-Jahren in ein Geschäftsgebäude für das 21. Jahrhundert. Oft kann nur geraten werden, welchen Nutzen ein Gebäude ursprünglich hatte: War das Wagendepot früher ein medizinisches Labor oder doch eine Metzgerei? AF

In architecture and town planning, reutilization has long since become a critical task. The reuse of existing structures corresponds to the imperative of sustainability, while the revitalization of historic buildings provides a sense of identity. Some images document far-reaching reconstructions, for example, the transformation of a brewery into an exhibition hall, the metamorphosis of a Wilhelminian-era shop into a gas station, of a grand palais into a bourgeois museum. Serious constructive retrofitting is required before an airy Expo pavilion serves as a museum, while just a few interventions transform a concrete-clad riverbank into a beach bar. Other images testify to temporary realizations, with an exhibition pavilion mutating into a mountain, a tunnel tube into a marquee, a highway bridge into a living area, a vacant ground floor into a hotel room. Some locations await conversion. Witness construction containers already positioned in front of an old market hall. Or is the neighboring property involved? Some architectural offices even reconstruct their own icons. In New York, for instance, SOM converted a bank building from the 1950s into 21st-century business premises. In some instances, one can only guess at a building's original function. Was this car depot once a medical laboratory or perhaps a butcher shop? AF

Foto **Photo** Bruno Klomfar, 2005
Ausstellung **Exhibition** Hans Schabus
Projekt **Project** Das letzte Land (**The last land**),
Österreichischer Pavillon Kunstbiennale Venedig
Austrian pavilion, Venice Art Biennale, kuratiert von
curated by Max Hollein, Venedig (IT), 2005

Foto Photo Manfred Seidl, 2012

Kunst am Bau Public Art Hans Schabus, Freitreppe

(Flight of steps), 2012

Architektur Architecture Dieter Mathoi Architekten,

Architekturwerkstatt DIN A4

Projekt Project Justizzentrum Judiciary center Korneuburg,

Korneuburg (AT), 2012

Foto **Photo** Eduard Hueber, 2013
Architektur **Architecture** SOM – Skidmore,
Owings & Merrill
Projekt **Project** Joe Fresh formerly Manufacturers
Hanover Trust, New York (US), 1954/2012

Foto **Photo** Margherita Spiluttini, 2000
Künstler **Artist** Michelangelo Pistoletto
Projekt **Project** Cittadellarte-Fondazione Pistoletto
in der ehemaligen Wollfabrik Trombetta
in the former Trombetta wool mill, Biella (IT), ca. 1870

Foto Photo Stefan Oláh, Champion,
Bartensteingasse 3, Wien (AT) aus from
Sechsundzwanzig Wiener Tankstellen,
Wien, 2009

Foto Photo Hertha Hurnaus

Ausstellung exhibition Absolut Wien Absolutely
Vienna – Ankäufe und Schenkungen seit 2000
Acquisitions and Donations since 2000, 2011

Architektur Architecture Oswald Haerdtl

Projekt Project Wien Museum (AT), 1959

226

Foto Photo Manfred Seidl, 2006
Künstler Artist Heinz Gappmayr
Projekt Project Raumtexte (Space texts), Haupt-
bücherei Main Library, U-Bahnstation Underground
station Burggasse-Stadthalle, Wien (AT), 2006

Foto Photo Margherita Spiluttini, 2001
Architektur Architecture Hermann Czech
Projekt Project Swiss Re Zentrum für den globalen
Dialog Swiss Re centre for global dialogue, Bar im
ehemaligen Pförtnerhaus Bar located in the former
gatehouse, Rüschlikon (CH), 2000

Foto **Photo** Alexander Eugen Koller, 2009
Architektur **Architecture** SHARE architects
Projekt **Project** Tel Aviv Beach, Wien (AT), 2009

Foto **Photo** Markus Kaiser, 2013
Architektur **Architecture** Maximilian Eisenköck
Architektur
Projekt **Project** studiowien, Wien (AT), 2013

Foto Photo Gisela Erlacher, Alfred-Grünwald-Park,
Wien (AT), 2001

Foto **Photo** Hertha Hurnaus, dwell magazine 09/2005
Land-Art Dani Karavan
Projekt **Project** Garten der Erinnerung (**Garden of memory**),
Innenhafen **Inner harbor**, Duisburg (DE), 1999

Foto **Photo** Paul Ott, Rinderhalle St. Marx,
Wien (AT), 2006

Foto Photo Lukas Schaller, 2011
Architektur Architecture Adolf Krischanitz
Projekt Project 21er Haus, Wien (AT), 2012
vormals formerly Österreichischer Pavillon
Weltausstellung Brüssel Austrian pavilion, Brussels
World's Fair, 1958; Museum des 20. Jahrhunderts
Museum of the 20th Century, 1962,
Architektur Architecture Karl Schwanzer

Foto Photo Markus Bstieler, aus from Unterinntal-
trasse, Wiesing (AT), 2009

Foto Photo Pez Hejduk, 2010
Ausstellungsansicht Exhibition view x projekte der
arbeitsgruppe 4 x projects by arbeitsgruppe 4 –
Holzbauer, Kurrent, Spalt (1950 – 1970), kuratiert
von curated by Sonja Pisarik, Ute Waditschatka, Az W
Ausstellungsarchitektur Exhibition architecture
polar÷ architekturbüro
Architektur Architecture Johann Bernhard Fischer
von Erlach
Projekt Project Hofstallungen, Wien (AT), 1725;
Umnutzung Conversion Messepalast, 1921–1995;
Architekturzentrum Wien, Fertigstellung Umbau
completed conversion 2001

234

Foto Photo Angelo Kaunat, 2011
Architektur Architecture kadawittfeldarchitektur
Projekt Project Salzburger Hauptbahnhof
Salzburg Main railway station, Salzburg (AT), 2014

Foto **Photo** Pia Odorizzi, 2009
Architektur **Architecture** Nickl & Partner
Projekt **Project** Studentenwohnheim **Student residence**
Albert-Schweitzer-Haus, Wien (AT), 2007

Foto **Photo** Stefan Oláh, Depot 52, Vorarlberg (AT),
aus **from** Museumsdepots – Inside the Museum
Storage, 2013

Foto **Photo** Zita Oberwalder, aus **from** Details
(Details), Dom zu Salzburg, Nordoratorium,
Salzburg (AT), 2014

Foto **Photo** Rupert Steiner, 2006
Architektur **Architecture** eichinger offices
Projekt **Project** Song Shop, Wien (AT), 2006

Foto **Photo** Pez Hejduk, 2005
Architektur **Architecture** Gerhard Lindner
Projekt **Project** Globenmuseum, Esperantomuseum,
Musiksammlung – Österreichische Natio-
nalbibliothek im Palais Mollard **Globe Museum,**
Esperanto Museum, department of music – Austrian National
Library in Palais Mollard, Wien (AT), 2005

Foto Photo Lukas Schaller, 2003
Architektur Architecture Lois Welzenbacher
Projekt Project Sudhaus Brewery Adambräu,
Innsbruck (AT), 2004, vor dem Umbau zum aut
durch prior to the conversion to aut by Rainer Köberl,
Giner + Wucherer

Foto **Photo** Dietmar Tollerian / Archipicture, 2009

Architektur **Architecture** any:time Architekten

Projekt **Project** Pixelhotel, Linz (AT), 2009

Foto Photo Gisela Erlacher, 2014
Kunst im öffentlichen Raum Public Art
Johannes Hoffmann, Johanna Reiner
Projekt Project Temporäres Wirtshaus Temporary
cafe, Sounds Against Silence. Stadt hören und
sehen, kuratiert von curated by Christina Nägele,
Ternitz (AT), 2014

Foto **Photo** Markus Bstieler, aus **from** Weyrer-Fabrik,
Innsbruck (AT), 2014

Making of
Making of

: Vom Nutzen der Mittel
: Uses of Resources

Wie gelingt das perfekte Bild? Da denkt man einerseits an die Beherrschung und die kreative Variation der technischen Mittel, ob digital oder analog, Spiegelreflex- oder Systemkamera, Mittel- oder Großformat. Mindestens ebenso wichtig ist aber die Arbeit mit den atmosphärischen Mitteln, die aus einem Schauplatz einen Ort, aus einem Haus Architektur machen. Was spielt sich rund um ein Gebäude ab? Welches Licht, welches Wetter braucht ein Bild? Wo sind die besten Standpunkte, wo die ungewöhnlichsten? Was soll gezeigt, was betont, was verborgen werden? Bei computergenerierten Bildern wie Renderings werden Sonnenstand, Schatten und Wolken, Perspektiven und Standpunkte, die perfekte Textur einer Fassade oder auch Menschen, die den Raum dynamisieren, aus digitalen Bibliotheken zugespielt und zu einer stimmigen Komposition zusammengesetzt. Architekturfotografinnen und -fotografen besuchen den Ort des Geschehens oft mehrmals. Diagramme erfassen den Lauf der Sonne; Skizzen halten das visuelle Konzept fest; Listen versammeln die Bandbreite der Ausrüstung, die benötigt wird. Und dann heißt es: warten, bis die Bedingungen passen. Das kann auch einmal ein improvisiertes Lager in alpiner Höhenlage erfordern.

Die Making-of-Bilder zeigen die Architekturfotografie als eine physisch anspruchsvolle Tätigkeit. Die technische Ausrüstung ist mitunter voluminös. Es gilt, unter Tische zu kriechen, an Abhängen zu balancieren und dem Tod durch Straßenverkehr mittels leuchtender Tücher zu entrinnen. Wenn Wohnzimmer temporär umgestellt oder ausgeräumt werden, produziert nicht nur die Architektur, sondern auch die Fotografie Baustellen. Erst im gelungenen Zusammenspiel der Mittel verwandelt sich die Dokumentation eines Bauwerks in Architekturfotografie. AF

How is the perfect image created? What comes to mind to begin with is a mastery of the technical resources – whether digital or analog, mirror-reflex or mirror-system camera, medium or large format – and its creative variation. At least as important, however, is the way atmospheric resources are deployed to fashion a setting into a place, a building into architecture. What transpires around a building? What kind of light, which weather conditions does the image require? Where are the best viewpoints, the most exceptional ones? What is to be shown, emphasized, and what concealed? With computer-generated images such as renderings, shadows and clouds, perspectives and points of view, the consummate textures of facades and human figures that serve to dynamize space – all are drawn from digital libraries and assembled into harmonious compositions. Often architectural photographers visit the location to be depicted numerous times. Diagrams capture the course of the sun, sketches record the visual concept, lists of the required equipment are drawn up. Then it becomes a question of waiting until the conditions are just right. Which can even require an improvised camp in the Alpine heights.

The making-of images reveal architectural photography to be a physically demanding activity. At times, the technical gear involved can be bulky. It may be necessary to crawl under tables, balance on steep declivities, escape death on highly trafficked streets by means of bright cloth markers. When a living room is temporarily adapted or emptied out, then not only architecture but photography as well produces construction sites. Only the successful interplay of all of the resources employed transmutes the documentation of a building into architectural photography. AF

Foto Photo Markus Bstieler, Arbeitsnotiz work note, Sölden (AT), 2013

Foto Photo Markus Bstieler, Arbeitsnotiz work note, Sölden (AT), 2013

Foto Photo Markus Bstieler, Arbeitsnotiz work note, Montafon (AT), 2013

Foto Photo Markus Bstieler, Arbeitsnotiz work note, Innsbruck (AT), 2013

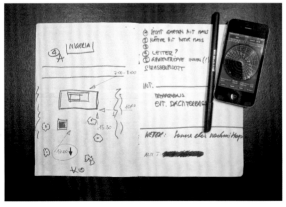

Foto Photo Markus Bstieler, Arbeitsnotiz work note, Wien (AT), 2014

Foto **Photo** Hertha Hurnaus fotografiert **photo-
graphing** Stefan Oláh, aus Ausstellung **from exhibition**
Guten Morgen, Stadt (**Good morning, city**),
kuratiert von **curated by** Manfred Schenekl,
Christoph Lammerhuber, 2014
Architektur **Architecture** Oskar Payer, Peter Payer
Projekt **Project** Wohnbau **Apartment building**
Siebenbürgerstraße, Wien (AT), 1964

Foto Photo Anders Holte, Fotoproduktion bei
Dietmar Steiner für photo production for NiVo
im Bild in the image Stefan Oláh, Nike Eisenhart,
Marco Walser, Manuela Hötzl, September 2013

Foto Photo Pez Hejduk, 2014
Architektur Architecture Anna Wickenhauser
Projekt Project Einfamilienhaus Single family house
K-L, Graz (AT), 2012

248

Foto Photo Inge Andritz fotografiert Hertha Hurnaus beim „liegend Fotografieren" photographing Hertha Hurnaus at "recumbent photography,"
Ausstellung exhibition Village Textures, Institut für Gestaltungslehre und Entwerfen, TU Wien, Wien (AT), 2014

Foto Photo Nicole Heiling fotografiert photographing Pez Hejduk, 2010
Architektur Architecture TU Technische Universität Wien, Institut für Tragkonstruktionen – Betonbau Vienna University of Technology, Institute of Structural Engineering – Structural Concrete
Projekt Project Egg-Grabenbrücke Egg-Graben Bridge, Großarltal, Pongau (AT), 2009

Foto Photo Markus Kaiser fotografiert photographing Markus Kaiser, 2015
Architektur Architecture Irmfried Windbichler
Projekt Project UBT Blutbank, Universitätsklinik für Blutgruppenserologie und Transfusionsmedizin Blood Bank, University Clinic for Blood Group Serology and Transfusion Medicine, Graz (AT), 2013

Foto **Photo** Sabine Jelinek, Landschaftsfotograf
(**Landscape photographer**), Lukas Schaller fotografiert
die Nekropolen von Cerveteri **photographing the**
necropolises of Cerveteri (IT), 2012

Foto Photo Pez Hejduk, aus from Donaucity, Wien (AT), 2003

Foto **Photo** Pia Odorizzi, 2008
Architektur **Architecture** ABH Generalplanung
Projekt **Project** Aspöck, Peuerbach (AT), 2008

Foto Photo Pia Odorizzi, 2011
Architektur Architecture Kiskan Kaufmann +
Venturo
Projekt Project Probebühne Wiener Staatsoper
Rehearsal stage, Vienna state opera house, Arsenal,
Wien (AT), 2011

Foto Photo Pia Odorizzi, 2012
Architektur Architecture Kiskan Kaufmann +
Venturo
Projekt Project Probebühne Wiener Staatsoper
Rehearsal stage, Vienna state opera house, Arsenal,
Wien (AT), 2011

Archivierung
Archiving

: Nach der Nutzung
: After the Use

Welche Lebensspanne können Gebäude haben? Lebensdauer ist nicht nur ein technisches, sondern auch ein kulturelles Phänomen. Wie viel leichter ist es, für den Schutz eines barocken Palais Verbündete zu finden als für Bauwerke der Nachkriegsmoderne? Werden Gebäude abgerissen, Fassaden überformt, Innenräume ausgeweidet, so werden die Fotos zu wertvollen Zeitdokumenten. Mitunter tritt die Architekturfotografie genau zum Zeitpunkt der Zerstörung auf den Plan. Was über Jahre geplant und gebaut und über Jahrzehnte bewohnt wurde, fällt innerhalb weniger Sekunden in sich zusammen. Oft stehen Gebäude längere Zeit leer, bevor sie umgebaut werden. Sie sind in Warteposition, verhängt von schützenden Gerüsten. Ist eine Architektur ohne Menschen noch Architektur oder bereits Skulptur? Die poetische Aura eines mit Brettern vernagelten Pavillons nach der Biennalesaison in Venedig, der verwunschene Ort einer funktionslosen Grenzstation suggerieren Letzteres. Was aber passiert, wenn das ehemalige Kommandantenhaus des KZ Ravensbrück zum liebevoll renovierten Museumsstück wird?

Das Ins-Bild-Setzen des Endes einer Lebensspanne bildet für die Architekturfotografie gleichsam den Gegenpol zum Fotografieren des Anfangs. Erst im Verlassenwerden treten die Einbauten, die im Alltag die Architektur überformen, deutlich zutage: die Kabeltrassen, Elektroschalter, typografischen Leitsysteme und Regalsysteme. Was erzählt ein Gebäude, wenn die Menschen fort sind? Der Blick durch das Fenster eines ehemaligen Kurhauses macht die Betrachterin zur Komplizin: Es gilt Abschied zu nehmen von der guten alten Zeit der Sommerfrische. Die Zeichen einer neuen Zeit, der (Rail-)Jet auf Schienen und ein funktionalistischer Kubus, haben sich bereits ins Bild geschoben. Zum Beruf der Architekturfotografie gehört nicht nur die Leidenschaft, Bilder zu sammeln, sondern auch die Aufgabe, sie zu archivieren und verfügbar zu halten. Sind Fotografinnen und Fotografen Sammelwütige? Fühlen sie sich deshalb zu anderen Sammlerseelen hingezogen, zu Depots und Archiven? AF

What kind of life spans can buildings have? Life expectancy is not just a technical phenomenon but a cultural one as well. Isn't it far easier to find allies to preserve a Baroque palace than to defend an architectural exemplar of postwar modernism? When buildings are demolished, facades reconfigured, and interiors gutted, photographs become indispensable historical documents. At times, architectural photography comes into play precisely at the moment of a building's destruction. In just a few seconds, a structure that was planned and built over a period of years and inhabited for decades collapses in on itself. In many cases, buildings are empty for extended stretches of time before conversion. They remain on standby, covered with protective scaffolding. Is a deserted work of architecture still architecture, or is it already sculpture? The poetic aura of a boarded-up pavilion after the close of the Biennale season in Venice, the enchanting site of a functionless border station suggest the latter. But what happens when the former commandant's residence at Ravensbrück Concentration Camp is lovingly renovated as a museum piece?

For architectural photography, the pictorialization of the end of a building's lifespan is essentially the antithesis of the photographic documentation of its birth. Only in the act of abandonment do the fixtures and installations that shape architecture in everyday life emerge clearly into view, the cable trays, electric switches, typographic signage and shelving systems. What does a building tell us once its occupants have taken their leave? A glance through the window of a former spa makes the viewer an accomplice, i.e., time to bid farewell to the good old days of summer retreat. The insignia of a new time, the (rail) jet on tracks and the functionalist cube, have already pushed their way into the picture. Intrinsic to the occupation of architectural photography is not just a passion for collecting images but also the task of archiving them and making them accessible. Are photographers collectors? Are they drawn for this very reason to other collector personalities, to warehouses and archives? AF

Foto Photo Günter Richard Wett, aus from
AnfangEnde – Abrisshäuser (BeginningEnd – Demolished
houses), 2005
Architektur Architecture Franz Prey
Projekt Project Villa Wierer, Kiens (AT), 1972,
Abriss Demolition 2005

Archivierung: Nach der Nutzung

Foto Photo Hertha Hurnaus, Fotoessay photo-essay in:
Weltkulturerbe in Österreich, Band I,
World Heritage in Austria, Vol. 1 voraussichtlich expected
in 2016
Architektur Architecture Franz von Krauß, Josef Tölk
Projekt Project Kurhaus Spa Semmering,
Semmering (AT), 1909

257

Foto Photo Stefan Oláh, aus from Österreichische
Architektur der Fünfziger Jahre (Austrian architecture
of the 1950s), 2009
Architektur Architecture Heinrich Hrdlička
Projekt Project Südbahnhof South station,
Wien (AT), 1955–1961

Foto Photo Stefan Oláh, aus from Österreichische
Architektur der Fünfziger Jahre (Austrian architecture
of the 1950s), 2009
Architektur Architecture Heinrich Hrdlička
Projekt Project Südbahnhof South station,
Wien (AT), 1955–1961

Foto Photo Paul Ott, 2003

Architektur Architecture Gustav Lassy,
VÖEST Systembau

Projekt Project Wohnbauten Housing estate
Harter Plateau, Leonding (AT), 1975,
Sprengung Demolition 2003

Foto Photo Bruno Klomfar, 2008
Architektur Architecture Michael Embacher
Projekt Project Filmarchiv Austria,
Laxenburg (AT), 2004

Foto **Photo** Pez Hejduk, aus **from** Wohnateliers,
Wohnatelier **Studio apartment of** Anna-Lülja Praun,
Wien (AT), 2001
Die Architektin Anna-Lülja Praun lebte und
arbeitete dort von 1964 bis zu ihrem Tod 2004.
The architect Anna-Lülja Praun lived and worked here from
1964 until her death in 2004.

Foto Photo Rupert Steiner, 2001
Ausstellungsgestaltung Exhibition design
Bernhard Denkinger
Ausstellungskonzeption Exhibition concept
Denkinger und Felber
Projekt Project KZ-Gedenkstätte Memorial
concentration camp Ebensee, Stollenanlage Tunnel
complex, Ebensee (AT), 1997

264

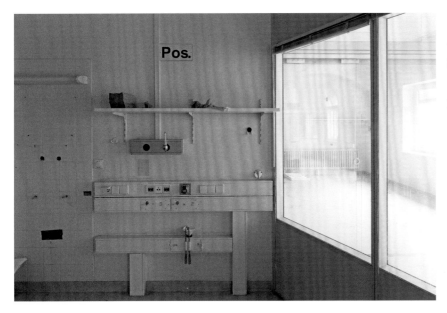

Foto Photo Günter Richard Wett, aus from
AnfangEnde – Abrisshäuser (BeginningEnd – Demolished
houses), 2014
Projekt Project Innere Medizin Süd,
Innsbruck (AT), 1953, Abriss Demolition 2014

Foto Photo Dietmar Tollerian / Archipicture
aus from Nach der Nutzung (After the use),
Tabakfabrik Linz, Kunstuniversität Linz, 2009
Architektur Architecture Peter Behrens,
Alexander Popp
Projekt Project Tabakfabrik (Tobacco factory
Linz (AT), 1935

Foto Photo Manfred Seidl, 2013

Architektur Architecture SS-Bauverwaltung

Projekt Project Führerhaus – eine von vier Villen

für SS-Offiziere und ihre Familien Führer House –

one of four villas for SS-officers and their families,

KZ Ravensbrück Ravensbrueck concentration camp,

Ravensbrück (DE), 1939

266

Foto Photo Margherita Spiluttini, Courtesy Christine
König Galerie, 1991
Architektur Architecture Emil Hoppe, Otto Schönthal
Projekt Project Hallenbad im Indoor swimming pool at
Südbahnhotel, Semmering (AT), 1882,
Umbau conversion 1932

Foto Photo Bruno Klomfar, aus from Transitory
Territories – Borders, Ottmarsheim (FR), 2002

Foto Photo Bruno Klomfar, aus from Transitory
Territories – Borders, Brenner (IT), 2002

Foto Photo Pez Hejduk, 2011
Architektur Architecture Georg Lippert
Projekt Project AUA – ehemalige Firmenzentrale
der former headquarters of Austrian Airlines,
Wien (AT), 1978, Abriss Demolition 2013

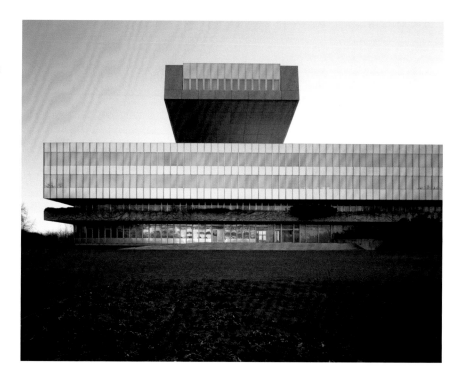

Foto Photo Pez Hejduk, 2012
Architektur Architecture Georg Lippert
Projekt Project AUA – ehemalige Firmenzentrale
der former headquarters of Austrian Airlines,
Wien (AT), 1978, Abriss Demolition 2013

270

Foto **Photo** Pez Hejduk, 2012
Architektur **Architecture** Georg Lippert
Projekt **Project** AUA – ehemalige Firmenzentrale
der **former headquarters of** Austrian Airlines, Wien (AT),
1978, Abriss **Demolition** 2013

Foto **Photo** Markus Bstieler, 2010
Architektur **Architecture** Massimiliano Fuksas
Projekt **Project** Palestra di Paliano,
Paliano (IT), 1985

Foto Photo Gisela Erlacher, 1994
Architektur Architecture Margarete Schütte-
Lihotzky, Karl Eder, Wilhelm Schütte, Fritz Weber
Projekt Project Schütte-Lihotzky Saal,
Schütte-Lihotzky hall, Globus Meldemanntrakt,
Wien (AT), 1956; Umbau conversion 1999

Foto **Photo** Dietmar Tollerian / Archipicture,
aus **from** Harter Plateau, 2003
Architektur **Architecture** Gustav Lassy,
VÖEST Systembau
Projekt **Project** Wohnbauten **Housing estate**
Harter Plateau, Leonding (AT), 1975,
Sprengung **Demolition** 2003

Foto **Photo** Manfred Seidl, 2013

Foto Photo Lukas Schaller, 2001
Architektur Architecture Erich Boltenstern,
Leopold Ponzen
Projekt Project Hotel Kahlenberg Wien (AT), 1935

Foto Photo Paul Ott, 2005
Architektur Architecture Ulrich Müther
Projekt Project Inselparadies (Island paradise),
Rügen (DE), 1966

Foto **Photo** Lukas Schaller, 2001

Architektur **Architecture** Sverre Fehn

Projekt **Project** Nordischer Pavillon I, Biennale-
Pavillon der nordischen Länder **Nordic pavilion I,**
Biennale pavilion of the nordic countries, Giardini,
Venedig (IT), 1962

Foto **Photo** Pia Odorizzi, Transport **Transport** aula
discorsiva – Halle für kulturellen und sozialen
Diskurs **(Hall for cultural and social discourse)**,
Heidulf Gerngross, Architekturbiennale Venedig
Venice Architecture Biennale, Venedig (IT), 2002

Markus Bstieler (*1970 in Brixlegg), bildender Künstler, lebt in Wien. Arbeitet mit dem Medium Fotografie seit 1985. Freie Arbeiten und Auftragsarbeiten in Galerien und Fachzeitschriften.

Peter Eder (*1950, aufgewachsen in Salzburg), Architekt in Graz. Fotografiert Architektur seit 1990, hauptsächlich für steirische Architekten. 1997 Ausstellung *Architektur ist überall*. Studienreisen Indien (Le Corbusier) und USA (Neutra, Schindler).

Gisela Erlacher (*1956 in Villach), Studium der Psychologie an der Universität Klagenfurt und Kamera an der Universität für Musik und darstellende Kunst in Wien. Als freischaffende Fotografin seit 1992 Arbeit an Projekten zeitgenössischer Architektur und Themen des urbanen und suburbanen Raumes. Publikationen: *cut* (2010), *Skies of Concrete* (2015). Einzel- und Gruppenausstellungen; u.a. in der Fotogalerie Wien, Galerie Fotohof Salzburg, im National Art Museum Beijing und Rezan Has Museum Istanbul; vertreten in Museen und Kunstsammlungen wie Museum moderner Kunst Kärnten, Artothek des Bundes, Artothek Niederösterreich, Artothek Wien und in privaten Sammlungen.

Pez Hejduk (*1968 in Klagenfurt), Architekturfotografin, lebt und arbeitet in Wien. FotografInnenlehre, Anlehre als Reproduktionstechnikerin. Langjährige fotografische Assistenz bei Margherita Spiluttini. Seit 1996 selbständige Fotografin. Arbeiten für ArchitektInnen, Bauträger, Museen, Ausstellungshäuser sowie für KünstlerInnen und DesignerInnen. Seit 2000 Mitglied im Künstlerhaus/Gesellschaft Bildender KünstlerInnen Österreichs, seit 2003 Sprecherin der ig-architekturfotografie Österreich und Konsulentin für nextroom – Architektur im Netz. Monografie *Pez Hejduk – vor ort_on site* (2012). Diverse Einzel- und Gruppenausstellungen, Publikationen in internationalen Zeitschriften, Katalogen und Büchern.

Eduard Hueber (*1948 in Wien), Architekturfotograf, lebt in Brooklyn, New York. Studium der Architektur an der ETH Zürich, Diplom 1975. Seit 1989 Konzentration auf Architekturfotografie. Die wichtigsten Kunden in USA sind Bentel & Bentel, Cooper Joseph, Fogarty & Finger, MetLife, Marble & Fairbanks, Perkins + Will, SOM Skidmore, Owings & Merrill; in Europa Baumschlager Eberle, Bétrix + Consolascio und Vehovar + Jauslin. Bücher und Ausstellungen für Campi + Pessina + Piazzoli, Baumschlager Eberle und Simon Ungers. Regelmäßige Veröffentlichungen in allen wichtigen Architekturzeitschriften.

Hertha Hurnaus (*1964 in Linz), lebt und arbeitet in Wien. Fotolehre in Linz, Meisterklasse und Meisterprüfung an der Graphischen Lehr- und Versuchsanstalt Wien. Fotoessays für Bücher wie *Eastmodern* (2007, Mitherausgeberin), *Raum verschraubt mit der Zeit* (2011), *Harry Glück, Wohnbauten* (2014). Diverse Einzel- und Gruppenausstellungen. Langjährige Zusammenarbeit mit national und international tätigen Architekten sowie zahlreiche Publikationen, u.a. in A10, architektur.aktuell, AIT, a+u, Bauwelt, dwell, domus, FAZ, Süddeutsche Zeitung Magazin, Die Zeit.

Markus Bstieler (*1970 in Brixlegg) is a visual artist who lives in Vienna. He has worked in the photographic medium since 1985 and produces independent and commissioned works for galleries and specialist periodicals.

Peter Eder (*1950, raised in Salzburg) is an architect in Graz. He has been photographing architecture since 1990, primarily for Styrian architects. His exhibition *Architektur ist überall* was shown in 1997. He has made research trips to India (Le Corbusier) and the US (Neutra, Schindler).

Gisela Erlacher (*1956 in Villach) studied psychology at Universität Klagenfurt and photography at the Universität für Musik und darstellende Kunst in Wien. As an independent photographer, she has been working since 1992 on projects dealing with contemporary architecture and urban spaces. Publications are *cut* (2010) and *Skies of Concrete* (2015). Exhibitions include the Fotogalerie Wien, the Galerie Fotohof in Salzburg, the National Art Museum in Beijing, and the Rezan Has Museum Istanbul; her work is represented in institutions such as the Museum moderner Kunst Kärnten, the Artothek des Bundes, the Artothek Niederösterreich, and the Artothek Wien, as well as private collections.

Pez Hejduk (*1968 in Klagenfurt) is an architectural photographer who lives and works in Vienna. She learned photography and reproductive technologies. She worked for Margherita Spiluttini as a photo-assistant for a number of years. She has been a freelance photographer since 1996, and works for architects, developers, museums, exhibition venues, artists and designers. She has been a member of the Künstlerhaus/Gesellschaft Bildender KünstlerInnen Österreich since 2000, a spokesperson since 2003 for ig-architekturfotografie Austria, and a consultant for nextroom – Architektur im Netz. Monograph, *Pez Hejduk – vor ort_on site* (2012). She has had various solo and group exhibitions and has published in international periodicals, and books.

Eduard Hueber (*1948 in Vienna) is an architectural photographer who lives in Brooklyn, New York. He studied architecture at the ETH Zurich, earning his degree in 1975. He has focused on architectural photography since 1989. His most important American clients are Bentel & Bentel, Cooper Joseph, Fogarty & Finger, MetLife, Marble & Fairbanks, Perkins + Will, SOM Skidmore, Owings & Merrill; in Europe, Baumschlager Eberle, Bétrix + Consolascio and Vehovar + Jauslin. Books and exhibitions for Campi + Pessina + Piazzoli, Baumschlager Eberle, and Simon Ungers. Regularly contributes to all the major architectural periodicals.

Hertha Hurnaus (*1964 in Linz) lives and works in Vienna. She studied photography in Linz; master class and Master Craftsman's Certificate at the Graphische Lehr- und Versuchsanstalt in Vienna. Photoessays for books such as *Eastmodern* (2007, coeditor), *Raum verschraubt mit der Zeit* (2011), and *Harry Glück, Wohnbauten* (2014). Various solo and group exhibitions. Many years of working with Austrian and international architects, as well as numerous publications, including *A10, architektur.aktuell, AIT, a+u, Bauwelt, dwell, domus, FAZ, Süddeutsche Zeitung Magazin*, and *Die Zeit*.

Markus Kaiser (*1974 in Bruck/Mur), international ausgezeichneter Design- und Architekturfotograf, lebt und arbeitet in Graz. Meisterklasse an der Akademie für angewandte Fotografie sowie staatliche Meisterprüfung für Fotografie. Seine Kunden sind nationale und internationale Designer und Architekten. Regelmäßige Publikationen in Magazinen wie profil, architektur.aktuell, Deutsche Bauzeitung und Büchern. Einzelausstellungen sowie Teilnahme an Gruppenausstellungen mit der Ausrichtung auf Fragen aus dem medienkritischen und konstruktivistischen Bereich.

Angelo Kaunat (*1959, München), lebt in Salzburg und München; studierte Physik und Architektur an der technischen Universität München. Praxis in Architekturbüros in Paris, München und Graz sowie als Modellbauer. Assistent für Lichtdesign bei Max Keller (Münchner Kammerspiele). Seit 1992 freischaffender Fotograf in Österreich und Deutschland. 2003 Ausstellung in der Galerie Ruetz an der Pinakothek der Moderne München. Zahlreiche Veröffentlichungen in internationalen Architektur- und Designmagazinen und Publikationen. Die Buchproduktion *Welt aus Eisen* (1998) wurde u.a. mit dem Preis *Das schönste Buch Österreichs* ausgezeichnet.

Bruno Klomfar (*1961 in Schruns), lebt in Wien. Studium der Philosophie, autodidaktische Beschäftigung mit Fotografie und audiovisuellen Medien; Kameramann bei experimentellen Filmproduktionen. Ab 1995 Spezialisierung auf Architekturfotografie; intensive Zusammenarbeit mit ArchitektInnen, Kulturinstitutionen und KünstlerInnen. Aktuelle Buchprojekte: *Dietrich/Untertrifaller* (2008), *Kunst am Bau – Kommunale Interventionen Wien bis jetzt* (2009), *Bau(t)en für die Künste – Zeitgenössische Architektur in Niederösterreich* (2010), *Houses of Hydra* (2015). Einzel- und Gruppenausstellungen, u.a. Aedes Berlin, Architekturzentrum Wien, Austrian Cultural Forum New York, Kunsthaus Bregenz. Beiträge in internationalen Magazinen und Büchern.

Alexander Eugen Koller (*1971 in Wien), freischaffender Künstler und Fotograf mit Schwerpunkt Architekturfotografie. Lebt und arbeitet in Wien. Studium der Philosophie an der Universität Wien und am Kolleg für Fotografie an der Graphischen Lehr- und Versuchsanstalt Wien sowie Studium bei Prof. Peter Kubelka an der Städelschule in Frankfurt am Main. Langjährige Zusammenarbeit mit renommierten Architekturbüros, Unternehmen und Institutionen; zahlreiche nationale und internationale Publikationen. Lehrt seit 2012 Fotografie und Multimedia an der Graphischen Lehr- und Versuchsanstalt Wien.

Zita Oberwalder (*1958 in Leisach, Osttirol), lebt und arbeitet in Graz; Ausbildung zur Fotografin in Lienz und Innsbruck; Meisterprüfung in Graz; Hinwendung zur künstlerischen sowie Architekturfotografie, ab 1985 Arbeit als freischaffende Künstlerin und Architekturfotografin. Zahlreiche Ausstellungen im In- und Ausland; 2012 Auslandsstipendium für bildende Kunst der Stadt Graz; 2014 Outstanding Artist Award für Künstlerische Fotografie des Bundesministeriums für Unterricht, Kunst und Kultur.

Markus Kaiser (*1974 in Bruck/Mur), an internationally distinguished design and architectural photographer, lives and works in Graz. Master Class at the Akademie für angewandte Fotografie in Graz, State Master Craftsman's Certificate for photography. Clients include Austrian and international designers and architects. Regularly contributes to magazines such as *profil*, *architektur.aktuell*, and *Deutsche Bauzeitung*, as well as books. Solo and group exhibitions generally focusing on questions of media critique and constructivism.

Angelo Kaunat (*1959, Munich) lives in Salzburg and Munich. He studied physics and architecture at the Technische Universität München. He has practiced in architecture firms in Paris, Munich, and Graz, and worked as a model builder. Assistant for light design with Max Keller (Munich Kammerspiele). Independent photographer in Austria and Germany since 1992. Work featured in a 2003 exhibition at Galerie Ruetz and the Pinakothek der Moderne in Munich. Numerous contributions to international architecture and design magazines and publications. The book project *Welt aus Eisen* (1998) was awarded Austria's Best Book Design Prize.

Bruno Klomfar (*1961 in Schruns) lives in Vienna. He studied philosophy, and is self-taught in photography and audiovisual media, and a cameraman for experimental film productions. Specialized in architectural photography since 1995, and has worked closely with architects, cultural institutions, and artists. Current book projects: *Dietrich/Untertrifaller* (2008), *Kunst am Bau – Kommunale Interventionen Wien bis jetzt* (2009), *Bau(t)en für die Künste – Zeitgenössische Architektur in Niederösterreich* (2010), *Houses of Hydra* (2015). Solo and group exhibitions include Aedes Berlin, the Architekturzentrum Vienna, the Austrian Cultural Forum in New York, and Kunsthaus Bregenz. His work can be seen in international magazines and books.

Alexander Eugen Koller (*1971 in Vienna) is a freelance artist and photographer with a focus on architectural photography. Lives and works in Vienna. Studied philosophy at the University of Vienna and at the Kolleg für Fotografie at the Graphische Lehr- und Versuchsanstalt in Vienna, as well as with Prof. Peter Kubelka at the Städelschule in Frankfurt am Main. He has worked for many years with renowned architectural offices, enterprises, and institutions, and has contributed to numerous Austrian and international publications. Has taught photography and multimedia at the Graphische Lehr- und Versuchsanstalt in Vienna since 2012.

Zita Oberwalder (*1958 in Leisach, East Tyrol) lives and works in Graz; training in photography in Lienz and Innsbruck; Master Craftsman's Certificate in Graz; orientation toward artistic and architectural photography; has worked as a freelance artist and architectural photographer since 1985. Numerous exhibitions in Austria and abroad. In 2012 she was awarded a Scholarship for Fine Arts Study Abroad from the city of Graz, and in 2014 the Outstanding Artist Award for artistic photography from the Federal Ministry of Education, Arts, and Culture.

Pia Odorizzi von Rallo (*1964 in Wels), seit 25 Jahren Architekturphotografin. Lebt in Wien und Oberösterreich. Meisterklasse an der Graphischen Lehr- und Versuchsanstalt Wien. Langjährige Zusammenarbeit mit international tätigen ArchitektInnen; Publikationen, u.a. in Architectural Digest, architektur.aktuell, Architektur, Home, Architektur & Bauforum sowie in Architekturbüchern. Lehrauftrag für Fotografie an der Universität für angewandte Kunst in Wien. Dozentin am fotoK, Wien. Diverse Einzel- und Gruppenausstellungen. Architektur zu fotografieren ist für mich ein sehr meditativer Prozess, in dem ich versuche, dem Klaren, dem Perfekten, dem Statischen der Architektur ein Gesicht zu verleihen.

Stefan Oláh (*1971 in Wien), lebt und arbeitet in Wien. Studium an der Staatlichen Fachakademie für Fotodesign, München. Neben seiner künstlerischen Arbeit und Publikationstätigkeit wie Sechsundzwanzig Wiener Tankstellen (2010), Österreichische Architektur der Fünfziger Jahre (2011), Stadtbahnbogen (2012), Fünfundneunzig Wiener Würstelstände/The Hot 95 (2013), Museumsdepots/Inside the Museum Storage (2014) fotografiert Oláh Bildserien für verschiedenste Auftraggeber aus den Bereichen Kultur und Wirtschaft. Außerdem ist er Senior Artist an der Universität für angewandte Kunst in Wien.

Paul Ott (*1965 in Kremsmünster), seit 1989 freischaffender Architekturfotograf in Graz; 2006 Lehrauftrag und Gastvortrag an der Hochschule Wismar. 2011 Buchpublikation PAUL OTT Photography about Architecture. Seit 2012 Lehrauftrag Workshop Architekturfotografie, Meisterklasse Fotografie Salzburg. 2013 Gastvortrag an der Staatlichen Akademie der Bildenden Künste Stuttgart, Architektur. Diverse Einzel- und Gruppenausstellungen, sowie zahlreiche Publikationen in internationalen Architekturbüchern und -journalen.

Lukas Schaller (*1973 in Lienz), Autodidakt, lebt als Fotograf in Wien; 1998 Schule für künstlerische Fotografie bei Friedl Kubelka in Wien. Er fotografiert Projekte im Auftrag und freie künstlerische Arbeiten. Langjährige Zusammenarbeit mit Rainer Köberl, the next ENTERprise – architekten, Wolfgang Tschapeller, Atelier Franz West. Einzel- und Gruppenausstellungen, u.a. in der Galerie Museum in Bozen, Architekturtriennale Mailand, aut. architektur und tirol, Fotogalerie Wien, Fotohof Salzburg, Wien Museum, Architekturzentrum Wien. Zahlreiche Publikationen, u.a. in Wallpaper, New York Times, Mark Magazine, architektur.aktuell, brandeins, Phaidon Press. Stipendienaufenthalte in Paris, Paliano und Rom.

Manfred Seidl (*1967 in Wien), Fotograf mit Schwerpunkt Architektur, lebt in Wien. Studium am Kolleg für Fotografie der Graphischen Lehr- und Versuchsanstalt in Wien; seit 1991 selbstständig tätig. Zahlreiche Publikationen in Fachzeitschriften und -büchern, u.a. Querungen Brücken-Stadt-Wien (2002), Der Wiener Justizpalast (2007), Österreichische Präsidentschaftskanzlei in der Wiener Hofburg (2008).

Pia Odorizzi von Rallo (*1964 in Wels) has worked as an architectural photographer for 25 years. Lives in Vienna and Upper Austria. Master Class at the Graphische Lehr- und Versuchsanstalt in Vienna. She has worked for many years with international architects, and has contributed to publications such as Architectural Digest, architektur.aktuell, Architektur, Home, Architektur & Bauforum, as well as to books on architecture. Lectureship in photography at the University of Applied Arts in Vienna; lecturer at fotoK, Vienna. Various solo and group exhibitions. "For me, photographing architecture is a meditative process through which I strive to endow architecture with expression through clarity, perfection, and static qualities."

Stefan Oláh (*1971 in Vienna) lives and works in Vienna. He studied at the Staatliche Fachakademie für Fotodesign in Munich. Besides artistic work and producing publications such as Sechsundzwanzig Wiener Tankstellen (2010), Österreichische Architektur der Fünfziger Jahre (2011), Stadtbahnbogen[x] (2012), Fünfundneunzig Wiener Würstelstände/The Hot 95 (2013), and Museumsdepots/Inside the Museum Storage (2014), Oláh creates photo series for the most diverse clients in the areas of culture and business. He is the Senior Artist at the University of Applied Arts in Vienna.

Paul Ott (*1965 in Kremsmünster) has been a freelance architectural photographer in Graz since 1989; in 2006 he held a lectureship and was a guest lecturer at the Hochschule Wismar. In 2011 he published PAUL OTT Photography about Architecture. Since 2012 he has been teaching a workshop in architectural photography and a master class in photography for WIFI Salzburg. In 2013 he was a guest lecture on architecture at the Staatliche Akademie der Bildenden Künste in Stuttgart. Various solo and group exhibitions as well as numerous publications in international architectural books and journals.

Lukas Schaller (*1973 in Lienz) is an autodidact who lives as a photographer in Vienna. Studied in 1998 at the Schule für künstlerische Fotografie with Friedl Kubelka in Vienna. He produces projects on commission and independent work. For many years he has worked with Rainer Köberl, next ENTERprise – architekten, Wolfgang Tschapeller, and Atelier Franz West. Solo and group exhibitions include Galerie Museum in Bozen, the Architecture Triennial in Milan, aut. architektur und tirol, the Fotogalerie Wien, the Fotohof Salzburg, the Wien Museum, and the Architekturzentrum Wien. He has contributed to numerous publications, including Wallpaper, The New York Times, Mark Magazine, architektur.aktuell, and brandeins, as well as Phaidon Press. Travel scholarships to Paris, Paliano, and Rome.

Manfred Seidl (*1967 in Vienna), a photographer with a focus on architecture, lives in Vienna. He studied at the Kolleg für Fotografie at the Graphische Lehr- und Versuchsanstalt in Vienna; active as a freelancer since 1991. Contributions to many specialist journals and books, including Querungen Brücken-Stadt-Wien (2002), Der Wiener Justizpalast (2007), and Österreichische Präsidentschaftskanzlei in der Wiener Hofburg (2008).

Margherita Spiluttini (*1947 in Schwarzach im Pongau), lebt in Wien. Seit 1981 freischaffende Fotografin. 2008–2011 und 1995–1999 Mitglied im Vorstand der Wiener Secession; 2000–2002 Gastprofessur an der Kunstuniversität Linz; diverse Auszeichnungen, u.a. 1996 Österreichischer Würdigungspreis für künstlerische Fotografie. Zahlreiche Ausstellungen, zuletzt 2015 Landesgalerie Linz und SK Stiftung Köln, 2012 Camera Austria, Graz, 2010 Fotografins Hus, Stockholm, 2009 Museum der Moderne, Rupertinum, Salzburg; 1991, 1996 und 2004 Teilnahme an der Architektur-biennale in Venedig. Zahlreiche Publikationen, davon mono-grafische Bücher: *Archiv der Räume* (2015), *räumlich* (2007), *Nach der Natur* (2002), Neue Häuser (1993).

Rupert Steiner (*1964 in Radstadt), lebt und arbeitet in Wien und Niederösterreich. Besuchte nach einem kurzen Studium der Geschichte und Kunstgeschichte die Graphische Lehr- und Versuchsanstalt in Wien. Seit 1990 selbständiger Fotograf mit den Schwerpunkten Architekturfotografie und Kunstdokumentation. Seine Fotos und Fotoessays wurden in zahlreichen Zeitschriften, Büchern und Ausstellungen gezeigt.

Dietmar Tollerian (*1970 in Salzburg), Studium in Linz und Zürich; seit 2000 als freischaffender Fotograf im Bereich Architektur/Design/Landschaft tätig; zahlreiche Publikationen in internationalen Medien.

Günter Richard Wett (*1970 in Innsbruck), Architekturfoto-graf, lebt und arbeitet in Innsbruck. Studium der Architektur in Innsbruck. Arbeitet frei zu Flüchtlingsunterkünften, aus-sterbenden Handwerksbetrieben, Architekturen am Ende Ihres Lebens, über den Kosovo und Armenien. Ausstellungen in Österreich, Italien, Schweiz, Türkei. Seine Fotos werden in internationalen Zeitschriften wie architektur.aktuell, brandeins, oris, geo, domus, detail, DBZ publiziert. Er füllt Bücher mit Bildern von Brücken, Holzfassaden, Kläranlagen und kaiserlichen Räumlichkeiten.

zur ig-architekturfotografie
In den letzten Jahrzehnten hat sich in Österreich eine facet-tenreiche architekturfotografische Szene etabliert, die mit der Vielfalt der österreichischen Architektur korrespondiert. Zur besseren Wahrnehmung der Architekturfotografie haben österreichische Fotografinnen und Fotografen Ende 2003 eine Interessengemeinschaft und offene Kommunika-tionsplattform ins Leben gerufen. Sie hat sich zum Ziel gesetzt, eine breite Öffentlichkeit für den kulturellen und ideellen Wert der Architekturfotografie zu sensibilisieren und über die verschiedensten inhaltlichen Aspekte der Arbeit ihrer Mitglieder zu informieren.

Mitglieder Markus Bstieler, Peter Eder, Gisela Erlacher, Pez Hejduk, Eduard Hueber, Hertha Hurnaus, Markus Kaiser, Angelo Kaunat, Bruno Klomfar, Alexander Koller, Zita Oberwalder, Pia Odorizzi, Stefan Oláh, Paul Ott, Lukas Schaller, Manfred Seidl, Margherita Spiluttini, Rupert Steiner, Dietmar Tollerian, Günter Wett

Margherita Spiluttini (*1947 in Schwarzach im Pongau) lives in Vienna, and has been a freelance photographer since 1981. From 1995 to 1999 and 2008 to 2011, member of the Board of Directors of the Vienna Secession; from 2000 to 2002, guest professorship at the Kunstuniversität Linz; recipient of various prizes, including the Österreichischer Würdigungspreis für künstlerische Fotografie in 1996. Numerous exhibitions, most recently at the Landesgalerie Linz and the SK Stiftung in Cologne (2015), Camera Austria in Graz (2012), the Fotografins Hus in Stockholm (2010), and the Museum der Moderne, Rupertinum in Salzburg (2009); and she has participated in the Venice Architecture Biennale in 1991, 1996, and 2004. Her numerous publications include the monographs *Archive of Spaces* (2015), *spacious* (2007), *Beyond Nature* (2002), *New Houses* (1993).

Rupert Steiner (*1964 in Radstadt) lives and works in Vienna and Lower Austria. After brief studies in history and art history, he attended the Graphische Lehr- und Versuchs-anstalt in Vienna. Since 1990 he has been active as a free-lance photographer with an emphasis on architectural photography and art documentation. His photos and photo essays have been published in numerous periodicals and books, and shown in many exhibitions.

Dietmar Tollerian (*1970 in Salzburg) studied in Linz and Zurich; active since 2000 as a freelance photographer in the areas of architecture/design/landscape; numerous publica-tions in the international media.

Günter Richard Wett (*1970 in Innsbruck) is an architectural photographer who lives and works in Innsbruck. He studied architecture in Innsbruck. Freelance work in the areas of refugee shelters, dying craft enterprises, architecture at the end of its lifespan, Kosovo, and Armenia. Exhibitions in Austria, Italy, Switzerland, and Turkey. His photographs have appeared in international publications such as *architektur.aktuell, brandeins, oris, geo, domus, detail*, and *DBZ*. He fills books with images of bridges, wooden façades, sewage treatment plants, and imperial spaces.

about ig-architekturfotografie
In recent years, a multifaceted scene for architectural photography has established itself in Austria, one that cor-responds with the diversity of Austrian architecture. In late 2003, to improve public perceptions of architectural photog-raphy, a group of Austrian photographers founded an asso-ciation and open communication platform. The aim was to generate a broad public awareness of the cultural and intel-lectual value of architectural photography and to disseminate information about the most diverse thematic aspects of the work of its members.

Members Markus Bstieler, Peter Eder, Gisela Erlacher, Pez Hejduk, Eduard Hueber, Hertha Hurnaus, Markus Kaiser, Angelo Kaunat, Bruno Klomfar, Alexander Koller, Zita Oberwalder, Pia Odorizzi, Stefan Oláh, Paul Ott, Lukas Schaller, Manfred Seidl, Margherita Spiluttini, Rupert Steiner, Dietmar Tollerian, Günter Wett

Angelika Fitz (*1967 in Hohenems), Kulturtheoretikerin und Kuratorin, seit 1998 eigenes Büro in Wien. Sie entwickelt Projekte an den Schnittstellen von Architektur, Kunst und Urbanismus für internationale Museen, Ministerien und Kulturinstitute. 2003 und 2005 war sie Kommissärin für den österreichischen Beitrag zur Architekturbiennale São Paulo. Zuletzt kuratierte sie die Ausstellung *Realstadt. Wünsche als Wirklichkeit* sowie die Plattformen *We-Traders. Tausche Krise gegen Stadt* und *Weltstadt. Wer macht die Stadt?*. Beiratstätigkeit, u.a. im wissenschaftlichen Beirat der Stiftung Bauhaus Dessau und im Beirat von aspern Seestadt. Internationale Publikations-, Lehr- und Vortragstätigkeit.

Gabriele Lenz, Studium an der Universität für angewandte Kunst und an der Akademie der bildenden Künste Wien; Konzeption, Herausgeberschaft und Buchgestaltung in den Bereichen Architektur, Fotografie, Kunst und Literatur; Schriftentwicklung; Signaletik und Corporate Identity; Vorträge, Lehr- und Jurytätigkeit; seit 2012 Büropartnerschaft mit **Elena Henrich**. Unter anderem ausgezeichnet mit der Goldmedaille im Wettbewerb der schönsten Bücher aus aller Welt, Staatspreisen und Auszeichnungen im Wettbewerb der schönsten Bücher Österreichs sowie der schönsten deutschen Bücher. Seit 2015 ist sie Leiterin des Universitätslehrgangs Contemporary Book Design an der New Design University, St. Pölten.

Elke Krasny (*1965 in Wien), Kulturtheoretikerin, Stadtforscherin und Kuratorin; seit 2014 Professorin für Kunst und Bildung an der Akademie der bildenden Künste Wien. 2012 war sie Visiting Scholar am CCA Canadian Centre for Architecture in Montréal. Sie kuratierte das Buch und die Ausstellung *Hands-On Urbanism 1850–2012. The Right to Green*, die im Architekturzentrum Wien sowie auf der Architekturbiennale Venedig 2012 gezeigt wurde. Ihre Ausstellung *Suzanne Lacy's Dinner Party in Feminist Curatorial Thought* wurde 2015 an der Zürcher Hochschule der Künste gezeigt. Sie ist Mitherausgeberin von *Urbanografien. Stadtforschung in Kunst, Architektur und Theorie* (2006), sowie *Women's :Museum. Curatorial Politics in Feminist, Education, History and Art* (2013).

Philip Ursprung (*1963), seit 2011 Professor für Kunst- und Architekturgeschichte an der ETH Zürich. Studierte Kunstgeschichte in Genf, Wien und Berlin und unterrichtete danach u.a. an der HdK Berlin, der Columbia University New York, dem Barcelona Institute of Architecture und der Universität Zürich. Er ist Herausgeber von *Herzog & de Meuron: Naturgeschichte* (2002). Zuletzt erschienenen von ihm *Die Kunst der Gegenwart: 1960s bis heute* (2010) und *Allan Kaprow, Robert Smithson, and the Limits to Art* (2013).

Angelika Fitz (*1967 in Hohenems) is a cultural theoretician and curator who has maintained an office in Vienna since 1998. She develops projects at the interface between architecture, art, and urbanism for international museums, ministries, and cultural institutions. In 2003 and 2005, she was Commissioner for the Austrian contribution to the Architecture Biennial in São Paulo. Most recently, she curated the exhibition *Realstadt: Wishes Knocking on Reality's Doors*, and the platforms *We-Traders: Swapping Crisis for City*, and *Weltstadt: Who Creates the City?* Membership in various advisory bodies, including the Scientific Advisory Board of the Bauhaus Dessau Foundation and the Board of Advisors of aspern Seestadt. Publishes, teaches, and lectures internationally.

Gabriele Lenz studied at the Universität für angewandte Kunst and Akademie der bildenden Künste in Vienna; designer and editor; concept, design, and production of books in the fields of architecture, photography, art, and literature; typeface design; exhibition design, signage design, and corporate identity in the art and cultural sector; lecturer, teacher, and juror; since 2012, office partnership with **Elena Henrich**. Honors and awards include Gold Medal in the annual competition Best Book Design from All Over the World; state prizes and awards in the competitions for Austria's Best Book Design and Germany's Best Book Design. Since 2015 she has been head of the unviversity course Contemporary Book Design at the New Design University, St. Pölten.

Elke Krasny (*1965 in Vienna) is a cultural theoretician, urban researcher, and curator; since 2014, she has been a Professor for Art and Education at the Akademie der bildenden Künste in Vienna. In 2012, she was a Visiting Scholar at the CCA Canadian Centre for Architecture in Montreal. She curated the exhibition/catalog *Hands-On Urbanism 1850–2012: The Right to Green*, which was shown in 2012 at the Architekturzentrum Wien and the Venice Architectural Biennial. Her exhibition *Suzanne Lacy's Dinner Party in Feminist Curatorial Thought* was shown at the Zurich University of the Arts in 2015. She is a coeditor of *Urbanografien. Stadtforschung in Kunst, Architektur und Theorie* (2006), as well as *Women's: Museum. Curatorial Politics in Feminist, Education, History and Art* (2013).

Philip Ursprung (*1963) has been a professor art and art history at the ETH Zurich since 2011. He studied art history in Geneva, Vienna, and Berlin, and has since taught at a number of institutions, including the HdK Berlin, Columbia University in New York, the Barcelona Institute of Architecture, and the University of Zurich. He is the editor of *Herzog & de Meuron: Naturgeschichte/Natural History* (2002). His most recent publications include *Die Kunst der Gegenwart: 1960s bis heute* (2010) and *Allan Kaprow, Robert Smithson, and the Limits to Art* (2013).

Dank an Acknowledgements to Hubertus Adam, Aperture Foundation Inc.,
Dušica Dražić, Judith Eiblmayr, Oliver Elser, Georg Giebeler / 4000architekten,
Christine Frisinghelli, Mathias Haas / Kaufmann & Partner Architekten,
Sebastian Hackenschmidt, Theresia Hauenfels, Marina Hämmerle,
Henke Schreieck Architekten, Otto Kapfinger, Fabian Knierim, Aglaia Konrad,
Rainer Köberl, Christian Kühn, Andreas Lehne, Armin Linke, Isabella Marboe,
Susanne Neuburger, Michael Obrist / feld72, Gerald A. Rödler, Simona Rota,
Hanno Schlögl, Franz Schuh, Söhne & Partner Architekten, Walter Stelzhammer,
Wolfgang Tschapeller, Roland Tusch, Claudia Wedekind

Herausgeberinnen Editors
Angelika Fitz, Gabriele Lenz mit with ig-architekturfotografie
Konzept Concept Angelika Fitz
Visuelles Konzept und Buchgestaltung Book design
lenz+ büro für visuelle gestaltung, Gabriele Lenz und Elena Henrich

Projektkoordination Project management Pez Hejduk, Hertha Hurnaus,
Bruno Klomfar, Stefan Oláh, Lukas Schaller, Manfred Seidl
Herstellung Production Katja Jaeger
Projektkoordination Verlag Project management publisher Katharina Kulke
Redaktion Editing Angelika Fitz, Lisa Wüllner
Übersetzung Translation Ian Pepper
Lektorat Copyediting Sarah Schwarz (Deutsch German),
John O'Toole (Englisch English)

Autorinnen und Autoren Authors Angelika Fitz (AF), Elke Krasny,
Gabriele Lenz, Philip Ursprung
Fotografinnen und Fotografen Bildteil Photographers picture section
ig-architekturfotografie: Markus Bstieler, Peter Eder, Gisela Erlacher, Pez Hejduk,
Eduard Hueber, Hertha Hurnaus, Markus Kaiser, Angelo Kaunat, Bruno Klomfar,
Alexander Eugen Koller, Zita Oberwalder, Pia Odorizzi, Stefan Olah, Paul Ott,
Lukas Schaller, Manfred Seidl, Margherita Spiluttini, Rupert Steiner,
Dietmar Tollerian, Günter Wett

Lithografie Lithography Manfred Kostal / Pixelstorm
Umschlagbild Cover image Stefan Oláh, Theseustempel Temple of Theseus,
Wien, 2012 (Ausschnitt detail), Lithografie lithography Roman Keller / Malkasten,
siehe Seite see page 37

Schriften Fonts Sabon (Jan Tschichold, 1967),
Univers 45 und and 55 (Adrian Frutiger, 1957)
Papier Paper Munken Lynx Rough, 90g, G-Print Smooth, 170g

Library of Congress Cataloging-in-Publication data
A CIP catalog record for this book has been applied for at the Library of Congress.

Bibliographic information published by the German National Library
The German National Library lists this publication in the Deutsche Nationalbiblio-
grafie; detailed bibliographic data are available on the Internet at http://dnb.dnb.de.
This publication is also available as an e-book (ISBN PDF 978-3-0356-0587-7;
ISBN EPUB 978-3-0356-0589-1).

© 2015 Birkhäuser Verlag GmbH, Basel
P.O. Box 44, 4009 Basel, Switzerland
Part of Walter de Gruyter GmbH, Berlin / Boston
Printed on acid-free paper produced from chlorine-free pulp. TCF ∞
Printed in Germany

ISBN 978-3-0356-0586-0

9 8 7 6 5 4 3 2 1

www.birkhauser.com

Gefördert durch Sponsored by
Unterstützt von With the support of

pro:Holz
Austria

Gefördert von